the Poets of the Great War

WILFRED OWEN

On the Trail of the Poets of the Great War
Great War

WILFRED OWEN

Helen McPhail
and
Philip Guest

Series editor
Nigel Cave

LEO COOPER

First published in 1998
Reprinted 2002 LEO COOPER
an imprint of
Pen & Sword Books Limited
47 Church Street, Barnsley, South Yorkshire S70 2AS

ISBN 0 85052 614 0

A CIP catalogue record of this book is available
from the British Library

Printed by CPI UK

*For up-to-date information on other titles produced under the Leo Cooper imprint,
please telephone or write to:*

Pen & Sword Books Ltd, FREEPOST, 47 Church Street
Barnsley, South Yorkshire S70 2AS
Telephone 01226 734222

Painting of Wilfred Owen by Charlotte Zeepvat. Kindly loaned by T and V Holt Associates from
their collection.

CONTENTS

INTRODUCTION BY SERIES EDITOR

This is the first in a new type of Battleground Europe book – a look at an individual. Much has been written about the War Poets and other significant literary figures whose work was moulded to a considerable extent by their service in the 'war to end all wars'. However, not so much has been written about their war service, and more particularly that of the unit in which they served. This books fills that gap, and places Owen's writings firmly in the context of his war service. The traveller to the Western Front will be able to trace his routes, find some of his locations and visit the graves of many of his friends. The narrative outlines the battles and events that were to be reflected in his poetry; the authors do not make the mistake of assuming that his emotions were uniquely a consequence of what happened in the war but give enough information to be able to refer back to the formative memories of childhood and peacetime.

The War Poets have shaped the thinking of much of the population about the Great War – generations, now, of school pupils have studied them as part of one examination syllabus or another, as well as their having a wider, adult appeal. There has been a danger of having history 'written by War Poet', one of the consequences, possibly, of the fashionable trend of imbuing contemporary accounts with greater historical significance than is justified. Of course these accounts are important; of course these men, and the experiences they underwent, are a vital part of the historical legacy of the war. But they are only a part, and should not be overestimated in their significance. After all, ninety nine percent and more did not write War Poetry, and Owen's writings, amongst others, were not all fashionable until the 1930s. I am reminded of a cartoon that portrays two soldiers in a trench, with shells and bullets flying all over the place. One says to the other words to the effect of, 'Of course I should not be here at all. I am not a poet.'

That said, Owen's poetry speaks to the emotions and it is founded on heart-rending experiences – not all of which he hated. This book, based as it is on the expertise of two people with great knowledge and feeling for Owen, places him firmly in his context and at the same time should ensure that many will come to some of the out-of-the-way places where Owen was in France and pay tribute not only to his memory but also to that of his fellow citizens who fell alongside him.

Nigel Cave,
Ely Place, London

DULCE ET DECORUM EST

Bent double, like old beggars under sacks,
Knock-kneed, coughing like hags, we cursed through sludge,
Till on the haunting flares we turned our backs
And towards our distant rest began to trudge.
Men marched asleep. Many had lost their boots
But limped on, blood-shod. All went lame; all blind;
Drunk with fatigue; deaf even to the hoots
Of tired, gas shells that dropped behind.

Gas! Gas! Quick, boys! — An ecstasy of fumbling,
Fitting the clumsy helmets just in time:
But someone still was yelling out and stumbling
And floundering like a man in fire or lime....
Dim through the misty panes and thick green light,
As under a green sea, I saw him drowning.

In all my dreams, before my helpless sight,
He plunges at me, guttering, choking, drowning.

If in some smothering dreams you too could pace
Behind the wagon that we flung him in,
And watch the white eyes writhing in his face,
His hanging face, like a devil's sick of sin;
If you could hear, at every jolt, the blood
Come gargling from the froth-corrupted lungs,
Obscene as cancer, bitter as the cud
Of vile, incurable sores on innocent tongues,—
My friend, you would not tell with such high zest
To children ardent for some desperate glory,
The old Lie: DULCE ET DECORUM EST
                    PRO PATRIA MORI.

7

INTRODUCTION

The poetry that came out of direct experience of the First World War is an unfailing source of literary interest, personal perception and creative understanding. It is also a source of straightforward information – about morale and relationships as well as events and reactions. Just as military reputations change over time, the pattern of literary taste and popularity, between what was best known in 1918 and what is widely admired (and taught in schools) many years later, develops and alters. The recognition of Wilfred Owen's poetry as an essential voice of 1914-18 is one aspect among many that reflect modern attitudes to humanity and warfare.

The account in these pages is based firmly on Owen's letters as well as his poetry, and on military sources – battalion diaries, regimental histories, trench maps, etc. Unlike many correspondents in the front line, Owen wrote vividly and honestly about what he saw and felt, and although his front-line experience was brief compared to the war years of many other officers, his personal reactions and emotion underlie his skill with the English language to recreate the past for us. Information is given at the end of each chapter on its specific relevant sources, but the book as a whole could not have been written without constant reference to the letters and poems. Details appear at the end of the book about these and other sources, and those who wish to investigate Owen's life and work in greater depth will find plenty of further bibliographical detail in the material listed.

Thanks are due to a number of people who have helped and encouraged the production of this book. We are grateful to Messrs. Chatto & Windus for permission to quote from The Poems of Wilfred Owen, edited by Jon Stallworthy (1985), and to the Owen Estate and Oxford University Press for permission to quote from The Collected Letters of Wilfred Owen, edited by John Bell and Jon Stallworthy (1985).

Illustrations: Birkenhead Leisure, Birkenhead Library Services (pp.13,120); M. Jules Delva, Ors (p.78); the family of John Foulkes (pp.87,112,116); Paul Gavin (p.21); the Imperial War Museum (pp.86,108-109); David Jones (pp.7,13,122); the Manchester Museum Committee of the King's Regiment (pp.46,47,93); The Ordnance Survey (p.50); Julian Putkowski (p.26); the Dean and Chapter of Ripon Cathedral (p.73); the family of Paul Seret (pp:55,58,99); Shrewsbury Abbey (p.15); Shropshire Records & Research (p.15); This England Books for pictures from 'The Register of the Victoria Cross' (pp.80,113); Yorkshire Film Archive (p.72).

Biographical Table

1891	8 Dec.	Tom Owen marries Susan Shaw
1893	18 March	Birth of Wilfred Owen, Plas Wilmot, Oswestry
1896	30 May	Birth of Mary Owen
1897	5 Sept.	Birth of Harold Owen
1897		The family moves to Birkenhead
1900	24 July	Birth of Colin Owen
1906		The family moves to Shrewsbury
1911		Wilfred Owen becomes lay assistant at Dunsden
1913		Feb. Leaves Dunsden, returns home, ill
		Sept. Arrives in Bordeaux to teach English in the Berlitz School
1914	March	21st birthday
	from June	Tutoring in a family in the Pyrenees. Meets French poet Laurent Tailhade
	December	Tutoring in an English family in Bordeaux
1915	May-June	Brief visit to England, back to France
	October	Returns to England, enlists in the Artists Rifles. Training in London and Essex
1916	June	Commissioned in the Manchester Regiment. Reports to 5th (Reserve) Battalion, Manchester Regt., at Milford Camp near Witley
	July-August	Musketry at Aldershot, then Farnborough
	September	to Oswestry
	Oct.-Nov.	Southport, Fleetwood
	Christmas	Embarkation leave
1917	1 January	Arrives in France. To Etaples, then to 2nd Manchesters near Beaumont Hamel. Into the line near Serre, rest, then in the line again
	4 Feb	Transport course at Abbeville
	1 March	Rejoins battalion
	14-15 March	Concussion following fall at Le Quesnoy-en-Santerre
	17 March	Arrives at 13 CCS, Gailly
	4 April	Rejoins battalion at Selency
	8 April	Battalion relieved
	12 April	Into the line, Savy Wood
	2 May	Evacuated to 13 CCS with shell-shock
	16 June	To Netley hospital, Hampshire
	25 June	Reaches Craiglockhart War Hospital, Edinburgh
	17 July	Contributes to *The Hydra*, becomes its editor

9

	mid-August	Meets Siegfried Sassoon, newly arrived at Craiglockhart
	September	Writes 'Anthem for Doomed Youth'
	October	Writes 'Dulce et Decorum Est'. Meets Robert Graves. Begins to collect poems for publication
	28 October	Three weeks' leave pending return to unit. November Writes 'Apologia pro Poemate Meo' and 'The Show'. To 5th Manchesters, Scarborough. Meets Arnold Bennett, H.G.Wells
1918	31 Jan.	Attends Graves's wedding. 'Miners' published
	March	To Northern Command, Ripon. Rents lodgings in Borage Lane. Writes 'Insensibility'
	April	Writes 'A Terre', 'The Send-Off'
	May	Meets Osbert Sitwell. Writes 'Mental Cases'
	June	Writes 'Futility', 'Arms and the Boy', 'The Calls'. Passed fit for general service. Rejoins 5th Manchesters, Scarborough. Request from Edith Sitwell for poems for publication in *Wheels 1918*. 'Hospital Barge at Cerisy' and 'Futility'published in *The Nation*
	August	Embarkation leave. Sees Sassoon, wounded and in hospital in London. Returns to France
	September	Writes 'The Sentry', 'Spring Offensive', 'Exposure' Rejoins 2nd Manchesters, move to prepare for assault on Beaurevoir-Fonsomme line
	1-3 Oct.	Objectives gained, captures machine-gun position, recommended for Military Cross
	5 October	Back to rest
	18 October	Moving forward
	30-31 Oct.	Battalion takes over the line west of the Sambre-Oise canal near Ors
	4 November	Killed on the canal bank
	11 November	News of his death reaches Shrewsbury
1919		Publication of seven poems in *Wheels*
1920	December	Publication of *Poems of Wilfred Owen*, with introduction by Sassoon

Chapter One

THE UNLIKELY ORIGINS OF AN OFFICER

When No. 4756 Cadet Wilfred Edward Salter Owen was gazetted Second Lieutenant on 4 June 1916 it marked the culmination of his rather unlikely transformation into a commissioned officer in the British Army engaged in the Great War.

By background and apparently by temperament and instinct, the 23-year-old Wilfred Owen was not an obvious candidate for military life. From his young childhood he was determined to be a poet, and although his work is now known as one of the supreme expressions of the inhumanity of war, he seemed destined to make his way in more peaceful ways, in a literary career or in the church.

Walk 1. Birkenhead. Birkenhead Central Library in Borough Road is a good starting point for exploring the area where the Owen family lived. The Library itself has a striking modern commemorative window over the stairs. From the front of the Library, turn immediately right into Shaw Street and again right at the end, into Whetstone Lane. Walk a little way up it and stop opposite Beechcroft; the new school next to it stands

Plas Wilmot, the Oswestry house built by Edward Shaw where his grandson Wilfred Owen was born on 18 March 1893.

Wilfred Owen in uniform, photographed in 1916 by his uncle John Gunston.

The Owen family, without Wilfred, in 1916: Harold, Colin and Mary behind Susan and Tom. Note the Artists Rifles' brooch which Susan is wearing.

on the site of Birkenhead Institute, the school that Wilfred Owen attended from 1900 - 1907. Turn right into Derby Road and continue to a cross road; No. 7 Elm Grove, up the road to the left, was the Owen family's first home in Birkenhead. Return to the cross roads and turn left along Derby Road. A short way along, turn right down Chestnut Grove, turn left at the bottom, and take the second turn on the right (across the car park) into Milton Road. No. 51, on the left, is the family's last home in the city. At the bottom of Milton Road, turn right into Dingle Road, left at the T-junction into Larch Road, then at the bottom turn right on to the main road. At the traffic lights turn right into Willmer Road: No. 14, a short way up on the right, was the Owens' second home in Birkenhead. To return to the Central Library, walk back down Willmer Road and turn right.

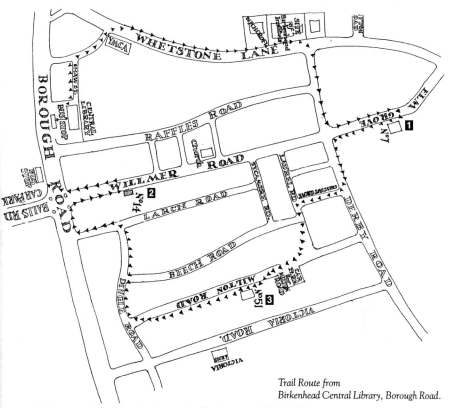

Birkenhead walk – the Owen family houses, 1897-1907

*Trail Route from
Birkenhead Central Library, Borough Road.*

**The Owens' houses in Birkenhead:
1, No. 7 Elm Grove; 2, No. 14
Willmer Road; 3, No. 51 Milton
Road.**

13

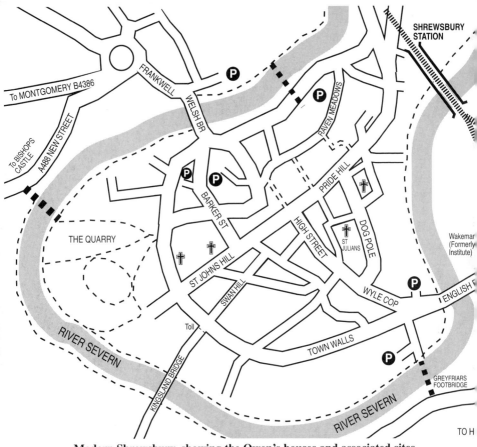

Modern Shrewsbury, showing the Owen's houses and associated sites.

The future poet had neither the traditional officer's public school education nor the experience of community life of the streetwise ranker or 'Pals' man of the First World War. In an age when social status shaped every aspect of life, the Owens valued their sometimes precarious financial and social position. His father, Tom Owen, rose through the railway world through a period in India and then posts in Oswestry (where Wilfred was born, in 1893) and Birkenhead, where the young family struggled to avoid being drawn into slum life round the docks. In 1907 he was appointed to the post of Assistant Superintendent with the Joint Railways (LNWR and GWR) at the important railway centre of Shrewsbury.

Walk 2. The Owens at home in Shrewsbury. Start at Shrewsbury Abbey (there is a large car park immediately across the main road), and look inside it for the memorial plaque near the west door, honouring men from the parish who were killed in the First World War and including

14

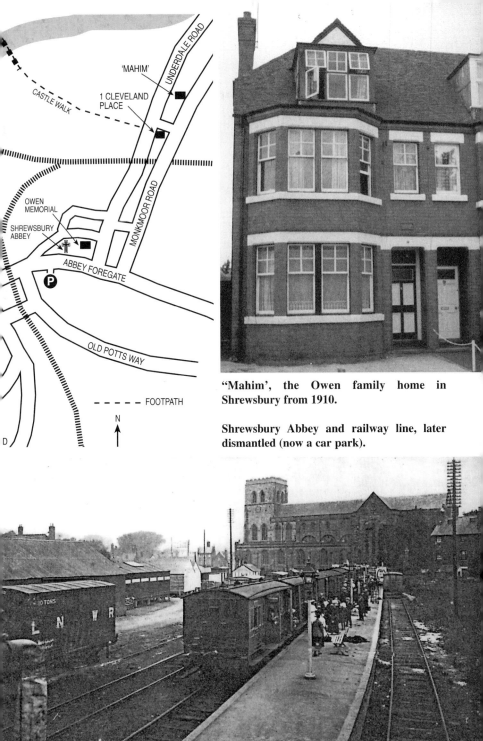

"Mahim', the Owen family home in Shrewsbury from 1910.

Shrewsbury Abbey and railway line, later dismantled (now a car park).

Wilfred Owen's name. In the Abbey grounds, near the end furthest from the river, the modern memorial to the poet is set in a circle of York paving, with an explanatory board close to Abbey Foregate. From the memorial, take Underdale Road to the left and walk along it under the railway line (the old halt used by Tom Owen stood beside this bridge) to the junction with Cleveland Street. The Owens' first home in Shrewsbury was in Cleveland Place, a group of four houses on the corner of Underdale Road and Cleveland Street: the name can still just be seen on the gate-post, almost obliterated by time and paint. A short way further along Underdale Road, No. 28 is the terrace house called Hawthorn Villa where Tom Owen's parents lived and where the young family lodged when they first arrived in the town. Walk up Cleveland

Shrewsbury station in the early 20th century.

Street and turn left along Monkmoor Road: the Owens' long-term family house is now number 69, but was then no. 71. A plaque over the front door identifies it as Wilfred Owen's home.

Return to the Abbey and take the English Bridge to cross over the River Severn, noting the Wakeman School on the right as you approach the bridge. This stands on the site of the old Technical Institute, the school where Wilfred Owen received his secondary education and where his brother Harold became an art student. In the town centre, St Julian's church (now a craft centre) has a brass plaque just inside the main entrance which commemorates parishioners killed in 1914-18, including Wilfred Owen. The Owens attended this church until they discovered the village of Uffington and took to crossing the river by ferry to attend the church there, but it was the Vicar of St. Julians, the Revd. N. F. Duncan, who on 31 January 1916 signed the certificate attesting to Wilfred Owen's good name as a candidate for a commission in the Manchester Regiment. The original handsome Victorian Gothic station building, where Tom Owen was Assistant Superintendent for many years, still serves rail travellers in Shrewsbury.

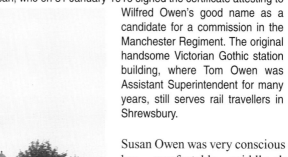

Susan Owen was very conscious of her comfortable middle-class childhood and education, and kept up her domestic accomplishments. Her family's prosperity dissipated by her father, she spent the rest of her life regretting the loss of her childhood ease and protecting her four children from rough, dirty or otherwise unsatisfactory friends and ideas. Wilfred grew up knowing about financial struggles, the importance of a steady job and the impractical value of literary studies in a sensible man's life; but from his mother, Susan, he also learned that religious observance and understanding was of central significance to life, that good manners, a cultured style and a

17

clean and neat appearance were essential for success and self-respect - and that she would support his determination to be a poet and man of letters at all costs. The adolescent Wilfred was a keen pupil at the Technical Institute in Shrewsbury (on the site of the present-day Wakeman School), enjoying the good grounding which developed his natural talents.

Tom's railway employment meant that rail travel was easily available. There were frequent visits to relatives, particularly to Susan's sister Emma, who was married to John Gunston and lived more prosperously than the Owens, first in Wimbledon and then near Reading. Father and son twice went on holiday to France during Wilfred's adolescence - the boy felt a strong attraction towards the country and the language. With the failure of his attempts to enter either a university or the church he took himself off at the age of 20 to Bordeaux, in south-west France, to teach English in a Berlitz school. His childhood ambition to become a poet was as strong as ever, although his loving but unsophisticated family life did not include any literary or strongly intellectual stimulus. Here, first as a hard-worked English teacher and then as a private tutor, he grew up and enjoyed the independence of young adult life.

It was also here that he met his first living poet, Laurent Tailhade, who praised and encouraged his writing and introduced him to the work of a wide range of other poets, French and English, living and dead. Here too he began to experiment with the 'pararhyme' use of near-rhymes which was to become a hall-mark of some of his most striking work. A series of such combinations can be seen in a poem 'From My Diary, July 1914' drafted in the autumn of 1917 but based on experimental lists of words noted in 1914. It opens:

Leaves
Murmuring by myriads in the shimmering trees.
Lives
Wakening with wonder in the Pyrenees.

and continues with this highly effective pattern of paired pararhyme openings to the lines and full rhymes at their endings.

It was from this distant region of France, exploring the Pyrenees and his growing creative skills, that the 21-year-old Owen viewed the outbreak of war in August 1914. Throughout his life he was an assiduous letter writer, particularly to his mother; she kept the letters and they now form a virtual autobiography, an essential and uniquely valuable background to the poet's life and work. (Of 673 letters and postcards that have survived, 554 were addressed to his mother.)

Perhaps inevitably, the war looked different from that distance and he was far from overwhelmed by the rush to enlist; on 28 August a long letter home stated that:

> *The war affects me less than it ought ... While it is true that the guns will effect a little useful weeding, I am furious with chagrin to think that the Minds which were to have excelled the civilization of ten thousand years, are being annihilated.*

He must have realised that this was an unusual approach, for he signed the letter 'Your own bundle of eccentricity Wilfred'.

None the less, he was forced to pay attention to the war by the presence, briefly, of the French government in Bordeaux. Until the threat to Paris was lifted by the first Battle of the Marne (September 1914), ministers and their entourage took over the city's public buildings, the Paris newspapers began printing there, even the national

Dunsden vicarage.

Mint was in operation there. And wounded soldiers were brought to Bordeaux hospitals; Wilfred was allowed by a doctor friend in one of the largest establishments to accompany him on a ward round and sent back some gruesome descriptions and drawings to his brother Harold. (This may indicate a lack of brotherly tact, for Harold was by now an officer in the Merchant Navy and sailing in areas patrolled by submarines.)

By the end of 1914 Wilfred was beginning to miss his home and family, and also mentioned worries about his health; this was not unusual, a habit he had learned from his mother - for Susan herself seems to have suffered frequently from vague or passing ailments, and many of Wilfred's letters express concern about her welfare. His attempt to enter the church, through working as a lay assistant to the Revd. Herbert Wigan at Dunsden, near Reading, from September 1911 - February 1913, had ended with a collapse which was both physical and emotional; he had returned home depressed and unwell, to be nursed and cared for by Susan, and the close relationship between mother and son was frequently expressed in their concern for each other's well-being. It was during this period that his sympathies for 'the underdog' became apparent; busy around the parish, talking with the old and the sick, the barely literate and the poverty-stricken, often in wretched cottages and enduring a prolonged period of agricultural depression.

Naturally enough for an adolescent much inclined to introspection and emotional expression, Owen's earlier work concentrated on his own feelings, and his admiration for poets such as Keats and Shelley; but the poem which begins:

> Deep under turfy grass and
> heavy clay
> They laid her bruisèd body, and
> the child

shows genuine concern for others and anger at the casual destructiveness of accidental death (written between October 1912 and June 1913).

Artists Rifles drill hall: showing their emblem of Mars and Minerva over the front door.

Now, in March 1915 in France, Wilfred confirmed once more his determination to pursue

20

Pictures shown in an Artists Rifles exhibition, 1916: 'Somewhere in France' and 'Untitled'.

The Artists Rifles former drill hall (now a dance theatre).

21

his childhood ambition:

> '*A boy, I guessed that the fullest, largest liveable life was that of a Poet. I know it now'*;

but three months later, after a brief visit to England, he asserted that:

> *I don't want the bore of training, I don't want to wear khaki; nor yet to save my honour before inquisitive grand-children fifty years hence. But I now do most intensely want to fight.* [c. 20 June 1915]

The smart and cheerful young man who returned from France in September 1915 brought with him a pile of poems, a good knowledge of the French language and way of life - and the knowledge that 'any gentleman returning from abroad' would be offered a commission in the Artists Rifles. Attracted by the notion of aligning himself with creative people even in such a destructive matter as the war, he presented himself at the unit's headquarters in Duke's Road, Euston

Owen in a group at Milford Camp, Witley, 1916.

Road, London WC.

Originally the 1/28th (County of London) battalion, (Artists Rifles), it became an Officers' Training Corps after successful initiation into active service in Flanders in October 1914. Its purpose was to provide officers for front-line duty as occasion demanded, while still retaining a proportion of men as a fighting unit to be called upon when necessary, and eventually provided some ten thousand commissioned officers. By early 1915 it had formed its third battalion, designated the 3/28th London, the unit that Owen joined in October 1915. Shortly afterwards it became the 2nd Artists Rifles OTC.

At first he 'lived out' near the drill hall, initially in Tavistock Square and then in Devonshire Street (now Boswell Street), and was soon writing home about the delights of typhoid inoculations, being kitted out and polishing his buttons, balanced by the pleasure of being based in Bloomsbury. One of his favourite haunts, Harold Monro's Poetry Bookshop, was also in Devonshire Street, conveniently close at hand for his intellectual and poetic support in between bouts of marching

and drill. Some of this was in Cartwright Gardens, close to the Artists Rifles drill hall:

We had to practise Salutes (on Trees) this very morning. You would be surprised how long it takes to do the thing properly.... It is really no great strain to strut round the gardens of a West-end square for six or seven hours a day. Walking abroad, one is the admiration of all little boys, and meets an approving glance from every eye ...
[2 November 1915]

A more traditional style of military life came soon, a barrack room in Hare Hall Camp, Gidea Park, in Essex, where Cadet Owen was posted to No.9 platoon of C Company. Given the demands and circumstances of basic military training it is hardly surprising that no poetry was written during his time in the camp (although some of his letters give hints of lines to come); it is tantalising to realise that Edward Thomas, another poet whose fame would spread far wider after his death, was in the same camp at the same time. The only literary respite was the opportunity to lodge at The Poetry Bookshop for ten days in February 1916, while on a course in London, when he was able to discuss his writing with Harold Monro and benefit from his experience and judgement.

Before his return to camp from the course, Owen was surprised to be offered a commission in the Lancashire Fusiliers: the heavy battles in 1915 - particularly Loos - had presumably created a shortage of officers. Conscious of his incomplete training, however, Owen turned down the offer.

In June 1916, as Second Lieutenant Owen, he joined the 5th Reserve battalion of the Manchester Regiment at Milford Camp, Witley, in Surrey, and wrote vividly to his mother about the men in his platoon:-

> *The generality of men are hard-handed, hard-headed miners, dogged, loutish, ugly. (But I would trust them to advance under fire and to hold their trench;) blond, coarse, ungainly, strong, 'unfatigueable', unlovely, Lancashire soldiers, Saxons to the bone.* [19 June 1916]

24

No poetry in this: but an attentive and perceptive observation of his men, an indication of the strength of feeling that would appear in his later writing about them.

Training at Witley and Aldershot brought triumph in his musketry skills, though there was also time to write a little poetry. (For example, 'Storm', which opens: 'His face was charged with beauty as a cloud/with glimmering lightning ...') In the autumn the Battalion moved to Oswestry, then to Southport as part of the newly retitled 5th (Reserve) Battalion, and on to Fleetwood. Owen was not much impressed by the pleasant resort of Southport, despite its suitability for training, with its broad sands, and his comfortable lodgings.

He was perhaps fortunate whilst at Witley to miss a draft that was posted to join the 1st Manchesters in Mesopotamia, an ill-fated theatre of war, but by the end of 1916 he was home on embarkation leave. By 31 December he was in the British base camp at Etaples.

Chapter notes and sources:

Birkenhead History Society

The Regimental Roll of Honour & War Record of the Artists' Rifles, Howlett & Son, 1922

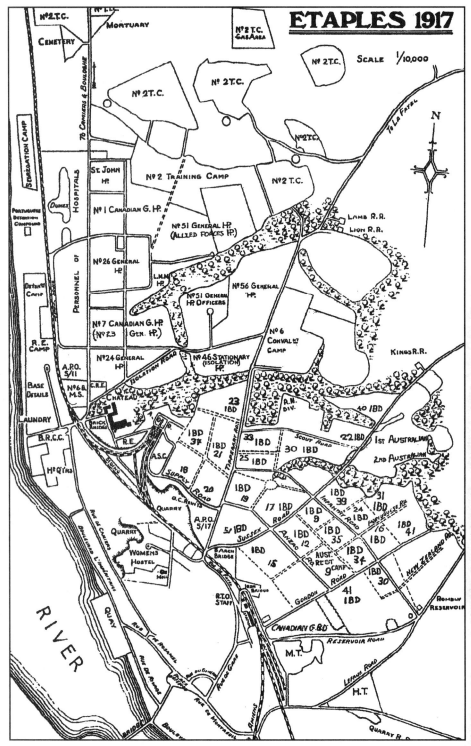

The British military camp at Etaples in the First World War.

Chapter Two

THE REAL THING

On New Year's Day 1917, Owen wrote to his mother from the British base camp at Etaples that: 'There is a fine heroic feeling about being in France' but three days later he had moved on from the base camp and discovered some less than heroic conditions:

'After those two days, we were let down, gently, into the real thing, Mud.' [Letter 476, 4 January 1917]

The unit that he was about to join, the 2nd Manchesters, had recently encountered more than 'Mud', for they had fought through the Battle

of the Somme since its first onslaught, on 1 July 1916, under the command of Lieutenant-Colonel Noel Luxmoore.

Lieutenant-Colonel Noel Luxmoore, DSO, Devonshire Regiment, attached and commanding 2nd Battalion Manchester Regiment, had quite an influence on Owen's career. Born in 1871, commissioned in the Devonshire Regiment in 1894, he rose to the rank of Major and then became Temporary Lieutenant Colonel in command of the 2nd Manchesters in February 1915. After being awarded the DSO on 1 January 1917, he returned to England in May that year at the age of 45 for staff duties and became Lieutenant-Colonel in 1919 and Brevet Lieutenant-Colonel in 1923.

Luxmoore went to France with the 1st Devons holding the rank of Captain. He was wounded at Vailly on the Aisne on 15 September 1914 (the battalion's first officer casualty), returned to the battalion in mid-November1915, and was involved in the battle for Hill 60. By October 1915 he was with

the 2nd Manchesters on the Somme with the rank of Major, and was wounded again. On his recovery he was made Commanding Officer of the battalion and led them on 1 July 1916 in their attack on the Leipzig salient.

According to Sergeant J. E. Prince, DCM, MM, serving in a 32nd Division trench mortar battery, Luxmoore was known as 'Corky' on account of 'his cork leg' - presumably the result of one of his wounds. The same sergeant described Luxmoore as 'a fire-eater' and although highly regarded by his men he was the terror of the battalion subalterns.

Heavy casualties led to this need for substantial reinforcements; for again, just as the end of Battle of the Somme was officially recorded, the battalion suffered particularly severe casualties in an attack on Munich Trench - part of a series of trenches on the edge of Beaumont Hamel. On 24 November it left the battlefield with only 6 officers and 150 Other Ranks.

This was the reason for the draft of 527 officers and men, including

Second Lieutenant W.E.S. Owen, joining the battalion at Halloy, east of Doullens, where the Manchesters were then in training. They moved forward, by means of what he describes as 'a redoubtable March' [7 January 1917] and bus transport, to Bertrancourt, which they found deserted, with no billets prepared. Owen's hasty letters home tell of cold, crashing gunfire, mud and intense activity. On reaching Courcelles the battalion became part of the Brigade Reserve. Conditions were quieter now compared to the preceding months, and the Regimental History barely mentions this period when Second Lieutenant Owen was learning about the realities of war: to the experienced eye, the battalion was merely and routinely holding a line of trenches in a sector where nothing much was happening.

Typical scene in the Somme area.
TAYLOR LIBRARY

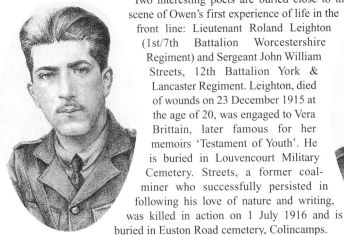

Two interesting poets are buried close to the scene of Owen's first experience of life in the front line: Lieutenant Roland Leighton (1st/7th Battalion Worcestershire Regiment) and Sergeant John William Streets, 12th Battalion York & Lancaster Regiment. Leighton, died of wounds on 23 December 1915 at the age of 20, was engaged to Vera Brittain, later famous for her memoirs 'Testament of Youth'. He is buried in Louvencourt Military Cemetery. Streets, a former coal-miner who successfully persisted in following his love of nature and writing, was killed in action on 1 July 1916 and is buried in Euston Road cemetery, Colincamps.

Roland Aubrey Leighton   **John William Streets**

Owen himself, however, was observant and learning quickly. His first choice as his servant was not approved, for the man belonged to the important bombing platoon and was therefore not available for officers' personal service. (This cost the man his life: as a servant he would have been exempt from most routine duties in the line, while his training as a bomber put him into the more hazardous positions.) His name cannot be definitely established, but he could have been either 41561 Private Tom Wood, or 41575 Private Thos. Wild - the only two men from Owen's company killed while they were in the line at this time. They are both commemorated on the Manchester Regiment section of the Thiepval Memorial, panels 13 and 14. Owen's alternative selection was a former chemist's assistant, who turned out to be

> *not only clean and smart, but enterprising and inventive. He keeps a jolly fire going; and thieves me wood with much cunning.*

[10 January 1917]

The 2nd Manchesters were taking turn and turn about on a two-company basis with the 15th Highland Light Infantry in a sector of the front line close to Serre, near a German strong point called 'the Heidenkopf' (known to the British Army as 'the Quadrilateral'). The actual length of front allocated to these two battalions stretched along the Serre road (D 919) and parallel with it, between the present-day Serre Road No.1 and Serre Road No.2 cemeteries. The Serre road itself was in No Man's Land, a shallow valley running between the British troops on the northern side and the Germans on the slightly

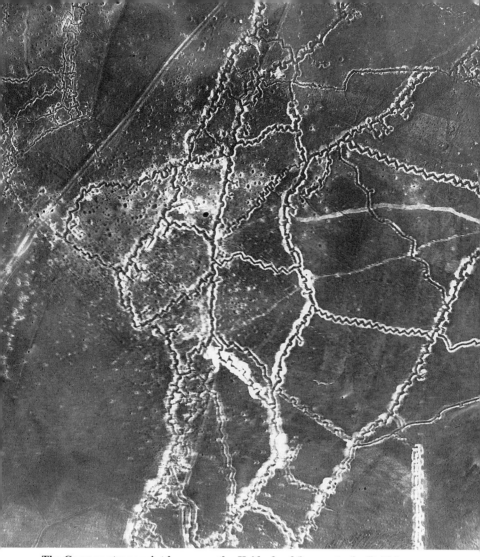

The German strongpoint known as the *Heidenkopf* (known to the British Army as 'the Quadrilateral'), which thrust out into No Man's Land.

higher southern side. This vulnerable position between the lines was occupied by one British out-post: troops were posted in a captured German bunker on the sloping southern flank of the road, about 40 yards from the north-eastern tip of what is now Serre Road No.2 cemetery. It was to this bunker that on 12 January 1917 Owen was ordered to take 25 men and occupy it.

His approach to the front line, beginning at Courcelles, was very literally down to earth, as he wrote home afterwards:

.. I am not allowed to send a sketch, but you must know I am transformed now, wearing a steel helmet, buff jerkin of leather, rubber waders up to the hips, & gauntlets. But for the rifle, we are exactly like Cromwellian Troopers. The waders are of course indispensable. In 2½ miles of trench which I waded yesterday there was not one inch of dry ground. There is a mean depth of 2 feet of water. [10 January 1917]

The photograph shows the ground the soldiers around Serre had to endure. Double belts of heavy enemy wire combined with mud and water made conditions almost unbearable. Several men were drowned in the attack on Serre. The photograph was taken in March 1917 when the Germans evacuated this section.

On 12 January two Companies of the 2nd Manchesters, with Owen in charge of A Company, followed a tortuous journey to relieve the 15th Highland Light Infantry. It took them through the ruins of La Signy

OWEN SPENT 'THE 50 HOURS OF MY HAPPY LIFE' IN A GERMAN BUNKER HERE, IN JANUARY 1917.

CORNER OF SERRE ROAD No.2 BRITISH CEMETERY

Serre road, eighty years after Owen 'suffered seventh hell' in the open field on the right.

Farm, where two platoons of B Company were left in the dug-outs as reserves, while two more of their platoons moved on down the trench to form an additional reserve in Basin Wood (see map). Owen and A Company continued down the trench system known as Sackville Street, where they left one Lewis Gun in an emplacement. At the end of Sackville Street Owen disposed his force, including several Lewis Guns, in the front-line trenches running eastwards and parallel with the Serre road, leaving an officer junior to him in command.

Taking two sections of his platoon, Owen took up his post in the former German bunker in No Man's Land: and until they were relieved

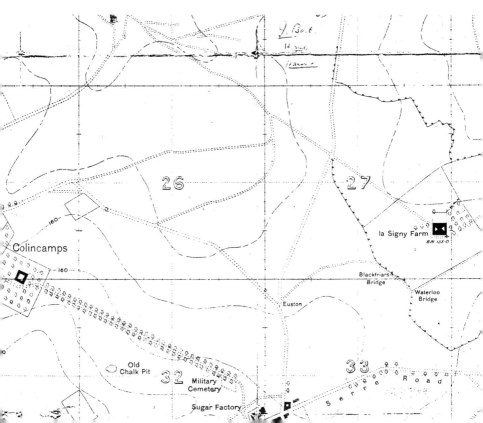

by the 15th HLI in the early hours of 15 January Owen and his men endured heavy enemy shelling, standing the whole time in some two feet of water with little headroom above them. Taking advantage of a lull in the firing, Owen left his bunker to inspect his other posts and crawled and waded 150 yards, a venture which took half an hour.

He found the experience of being under fire a shattering one and, as one of the few who did not want to keep family at home in ignorance, he wrote to his mother on 16 January:

> *I can see no excuse for deceiving you about these last 4 days.*
> *I have suffered seventh hell.*
> *I have not been at the front.*
> *I have been in front of it.*
> *I held an advanced post, that is, a 'dug-out' in the middle of No Man's Land.*
>
> *We had a march of 3 miles over shelled road then nearly 3 along a flooded trench... It was of course dark, too dark, and the ground was not mud, not sloppy mud, but an octopus of sucking clay, 3, 4 and 5 feet deep, relieved only by craters full of water. Men have been known to drown in them.*
>
> *... My dug-out held 25 men tight packed. Water filled it to a depth of 1 or 2 feet, leaving say 4 feet of air.*

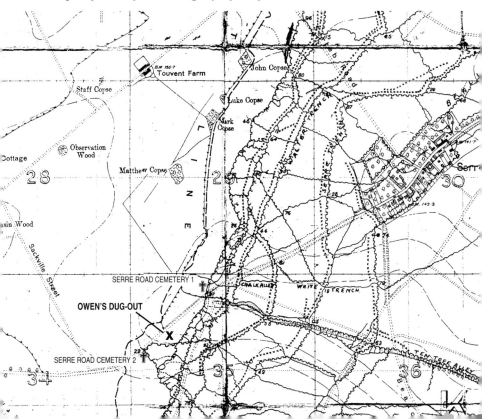

One entrance had been blown in and blocked.
So far, the other remained.
The Germans knew we were staying there and decided we
shouldn't.
Those fifty hours were the agony of my happy life...
I nearly broke down and let myself drown in the water that
was now slowly rising over my knees...
In the Platoon on my left the sentries over the dug-out were
blown to nothing. One of these poor fellows was my first servant
whom I rejected... I kept my own sentries half way down the
stairs during the more terrific bombardment. In spite of this, one
lad was blown down and, I am afraid, blinded. [16 January 1917]
At this period, poetry was not the foremost element in Owen's life; he
had no thought of writing about the war, and in any case conditions
were scarcely suitable for the necessary concentration and reflection.
Letters home were different, and it seemed almost as important to send
them as to receive news and reassurance from his mother; he regarded
his letters as his diary of the war and asked her to keep them, even
when they were to be kept away from other eyes. As soon as he began
to use his war experience in his poetry, however, this early incident of
seeing a sentry blinded - and knowing that another two were killed
nearby - became the foundation of 'The Sentry', first drafted between
August and October 1917. It opens:
We'd found an old Boche dug-out, and he knew
And gave us hell; for shell on frantic shell
Lit full on top, but never quite burst through ...
In the midst of the danger and discomfort, Owen was able to bring out
the Lewis Guns with his Company - in contrast, he asserts, to one of
the 15th HLI officers who relieved the Manchesters.

Walk - park in front of Serre Road No. 2 cemetery and walk a little
way up the field track on the opposite side of the road about 100 yards
to the west. This is the line of the British army's Sackville Street, with
Basin Wood further up it to the left and La Signy farm beyond.Returning
to the road, walk about 40-50 yards towards the village of Serre. You are
now in the middle of No Man's Land, with the location of the old German
bunker some 30 yards up the slope to the right of the road (facing
towards Serre). No trace remains of any concrete construction here, but
it is possible to see how dangerous and exposed it must have felt; this
is a good place to read Owen's letter of 16 January 1917, and his poem
'The Sentry'.

Despite a claim in the letter of 16 January that they were **'never going**

A wounded soldier crawls back to his snow covered trench.

back to this awful place' (Owen's emphasis), the 'worst the Manchesters have ever held', and another letter three days later in which he describes their conditions as 'wretched beyond my previous imagination', he was soon back in the front line. On 23 January the 2nd Manchesters moved to new positions nearer Beaumont Hamel and towards Munich Trench, in which they were overlooked by the enemy. Battalion headquarters was to their rear, in the White City. In this notoriously cold winter, the frost descended on the men who were lying out in the snow and 'deadly wind'; they had no dug-outs and as they were under observation they could not move in daylight hours:

> *We had 5 Tommy's cookers between the Platoon, but they did not suffice to melt the ice in the water-cans. So we suffered cruelly from thirst. The marvel is that we did not all die of cold.*

This photograph illustrates the conditions endured by soldiers of both sides during the winter of 1916/17.

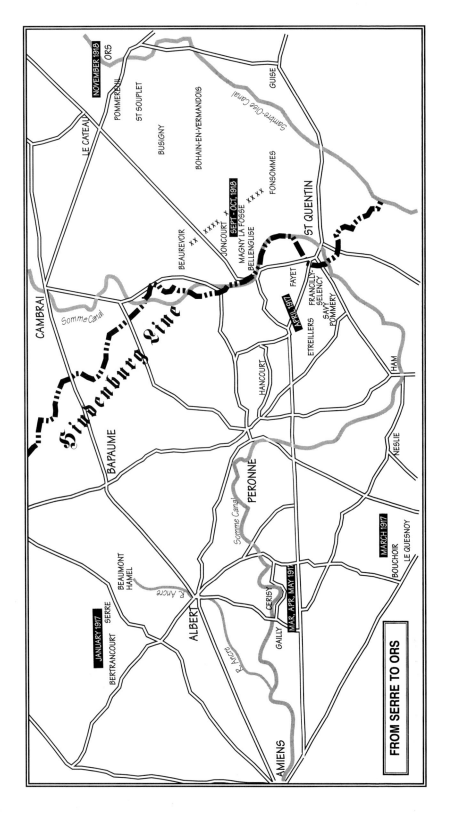

FROM SERRE TO ORS

The N29 between Amiens and St Quentin. Despite its battered state, the road became one of the principal routes used in the British advance during March and April 1917.

> *.. only one of my party actually froze to death before he could be got back... My feet ached until they could ache no more, and so they temporarily died. I was kept warm by the ardour of Life within me.* [4 February 1917]

He had also encountered a whiff of gas, and a view of the terrain of war that echoed the Biblical teaching of his childhood:

> *They want to call No Man's Land 'England' because we keep supremacy there. It is like the eternal place of gnashing of teeth; the Slough of Despond could be contained in one of its crater-holes; the fires of Sodom and Gomorrah could not light a candle to it - to find the way to Babylon the Fallen. It is pock-marked like a body of foulest disease and its odour is the breath of cancer...* [19 January 1917]

He was remarkably frank in describing the effect of the war on his own feelings, once again using his poet's inner eye:

> *I suppose I can endure cold, and fatigue, and the face-to-face death, as well as another; but extra for me there is the universal pervasion of Ugliness. Hideous landscapes, vile noises, foul language, and nothing but foul, even from one's own mouth (for all are devil ridden), everything unnatural, broken, blasted; the distortion of the dead, whose unburiable bodies sit outside the dug-outs all day, all night, the most execrable sights on earth. In poetry we call them the most glorious. But to sit with them all day, all night ... and a week later to come back and find them still sitting there, in motionless groups, THAT is what saps the 'soldierly spirit'...* [4 February 1917]

From the Battalion's rest base at Bertrancourt, Owen was sent on a three-week Army Transport course at Abbeville, a pleasant change in

Post-war reconstruction: Bouchoir Mairie and school, rebuilt after the damage of the First World War.

an attractive rear area. Here he had time for 'a little verse' once more; a product of this period was 'Happiness', one of several poems written on a subject agreed by Owen, his cousin Leslie Gunston and their friend Olwen Joergens. The course meant that he was absent from the line when the Germans unexpectedly began to withdraw eastwards to their new defensive system, the Hindenburg Line. The British Army advanced in their wake; the 2nd Manchesters headed south from Bertrancourt, crossed the River Somme and took over from the French in the front line near Le Quesnoy en Santerre. Battalion HQ was established in the shell-damaged village of Bouchoir on the Amiens-Noyon road. This was where he caught up with the Battalion once more.

This time he joined B Company, which he found more congenial than the A Company posting - a state of affairs that he attributed to the sergeants and his new and very efficient Company Commander, Lieutenant S. Sorrel. (Sorrel was invalided home a few weeks later with shell-shock. Owen refers to him as a poet, but nothing of his work has ever been identified.) Le Quesnoy was one of the villages in their sector, in ruins and close to the front line.[1] Working parties were set to work building dug-outs; and a letter from Owen, which has not survived but which was quoted by Edmund Blunden in his 1931 memoir, described an incident there:

> Last night I was going round through pitch darkness to see a man in a dangerous state of exhaustion. I fell into a kind of well, only about 15 ft., but I caught the back of my head on the way down. The doctors (not in consultation!) say I have a slight concussion. [14 March 1917]

He was sent to 13 Casualty Clearing Station at Gailly, north-east of Villers-Bretoneux on the canalised River Somme, and when he wrote to his mother a few days later he had sufficiently recovered from the

1. Post-war reconstruction has left little trace of the war here, but trench lines can be seen in a small copse, between Le Quesnoy and Damery.

Site of 13 CCS, front, with the Somme canal hidden in the line of trees.

initial vomiting and headache to give a clear-eyed description of conditions there:

> *Sometimes a Sister blows in to this ward, and flutes a bit on a high voice, or pegs around on a high heel, but we are really attended by orderlies, who are fresh & clean, and much preferable, being not only serener and sensibler, but also private soldiers with no airs of authority about 'em.* [18 March 1917 - his 24th birthday]

The unit was a mass of huts and tents covering a large field close to the locks on the canalised River Somme, and commanded by Lieutenant-Colonel Ellery of the Royal Army Medical Corps. When Owen arrived there it held some 600 patients. It was connected by a railway line which ran to the south to sidings near the main railway line at Marcelcave, on the Amiens - Nesle line. As usual, the less-seriously ill patients helped to look after those in a worse condition than themselves - such as the two Royal Flying Corps officers who were 'terribly smashed', as Owen described it. One, a pilot, told him about a friend from his days at Dunsden vicarage, Lieutenant A. E. Boultbee. Described by the pilot as 'a very wild fellow', Boultbee was shot down over the German lines by Baron von Richthofen on the day of Owen's arrival at the CCS (17 March 1917).

Trees felled by the Germans at Péronne in order to obstruct the road

The German army was removing its men and matériel eastwards to its new defensive system. As it shifted eastwards to the Hindenburg Line - which was still being constructed, with the unwilling help of French civilian labour gangs - they stopped to fight a rearguard action when they were hard-pressed or needed to gain time. As part of the planned operation to hinder the Allies advancing behind them, the land was laid waste, villages destroyed, wells blocked or destroyed and booby traps set up. As a result, the British army was forced to spend considerable time in clearing the ground and building roads and bridges.

As the Manchesters pressed forward they encountered French civilians delighted to be liberated from their oppressive occupation - in the town of Nesle, for example, where cavalry units of King Edward's Horse entered on 18 March 1917, followed the next day by the 16th Highland Light Infantry. Local delight among the women, children and older men left behind by the enemy was tempered by their distress at the removal of older boys and girls who had been taken by the retreating Germans. It was with some difficulty that the Highlanders prevented the population from killing German prisoners.

British support services moved into Nesle promptly and set up medical facilities in the town's Hospice, or public hospital, for the wounded soldiers who were soon coming down from the St. Quentin front; and the French President, Raymond Poincaré, visited the town and saw the 16th HLI before they continued their advance towards St. Quentin. The troops immediately began to restore rail and road communications.

Nesle is an attractive small town and its cemetery is worth a visit. It is not far from the town centre, towards the eastern edge and near the old Hospice, which is where Owen stayed early in April 1917 (see below). The British plot in the cemetery is in three rows, with the graves of 135 soldiers, including a number of 2nd Manchesters and 15th and 16th Lancashire Fusiliers men. They were wounded in the battles at Savy and Francilly-Selency and died in hospital in Nesle.

Meanwhile, the concussed Second Lieutenant Owen was observing life from his hospital bed in 13 CCS or sitting round the ward stove. He concentrated his attention on drawing plans for country houses, particularly the ideal bungalow for his own use; he thought about his young brother Colin (working for a farmer near Shrewsbury) and proclaimed his ambition to keep pigs after the war - a cottage in Kent,

British Engineers bringing up pontoons to bridge the river in Nesle, where Owen stayed.

Surrey or Sussex with an orchard would suit his purpose. The letter which described this idyllic future included a poem, 'Sonnet - with an identity disc'[2] A few days later, when he was sufficiently recovered to beg 'a joy ride' in a motor ambulance, he described a conversation with refugees from the regained area. A boy of 14, thin and barely literate after 2½ years of German occupation, described how the retreating Germans had

> ... *carried off all men over 15; left 5 days bread rations for the remainder, set fire to almost every building, choked up the wells with farmyard refuse and disappeared.* [25 March 1917].

At the end of March, Owen was discharged from the CCS and set off to rejoin his unit, catching up with them at Beauvois while they were involved in Brigade attacks on the Hindenburg Line in front of St. Quentin. Perhaps as a result of the concussion, Owen appears later to have referred to his movements to and from the CCS in March in somewhat confusing terms. His letter home on 18 March refers to being 'sent to a shanty a bit further back': this is annotated in his Collected Letters as being the Military Hospital at Nesle, linked to a comment a year later (31 March 1918) that 'Even Nesle, a town

43

2. Lines from this sonnet are included in the Western Front Association memorial plaque beside the canal bridge at Ors.

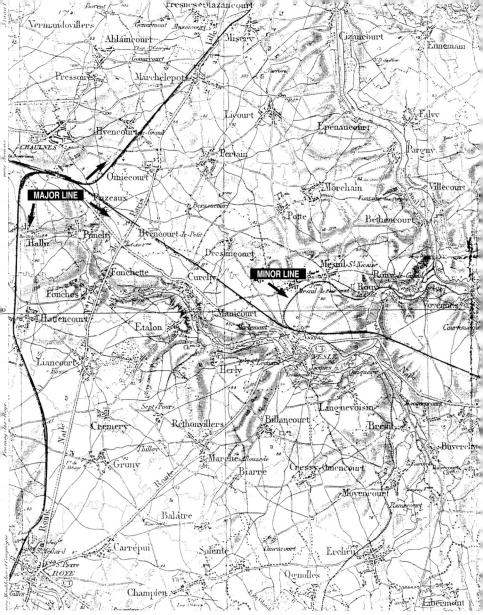

The French railway network south-west of St. Quentin in the First World War period.

hospital where I paused 3 days, is occupied'. It was on 16 March that he was sent back from the line, arriving at 13 CCS the next day - but Nesle was not liberated until 18 March. It seems therefore that it was on his journey back to his unit, after recovering, that he stayed in

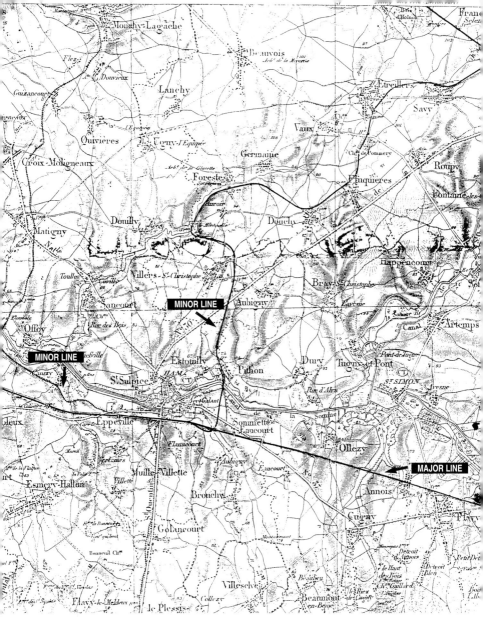

Nesle, presumably waiting for transport - the railway network here was a significant feature in the movement of troops and stores to and from the front line in the St. Quentin area.

The battlefield that concerned the 2nd Manchesters lay immediately to the south of the main road from Amiens as it approached St. Quentin, between the straight road running south from Holnon to Savy

Defences round St Quentin in 1917: (a) two Manchester Regiment trench maps, 31.3.17.

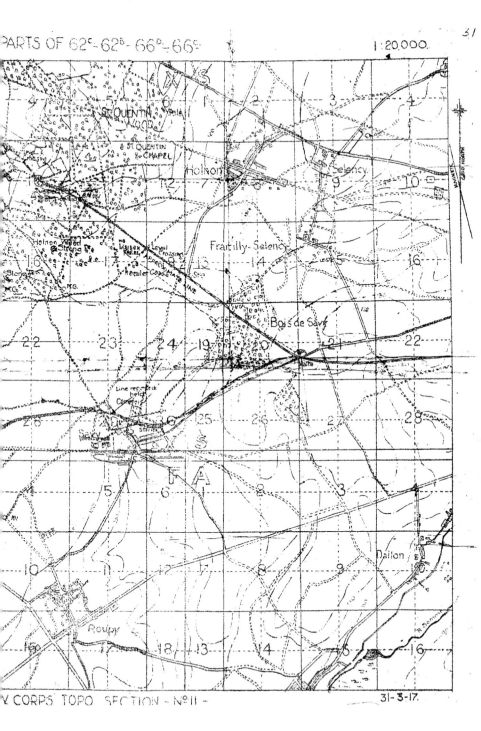

PARTS OF 62ᶜ·62ᵇ·66ᵇ·66ᵈ

1:20,000.

and the road from Selency to the Savy - St. Quentin road. Beside the junction of these two roads lay the German strong-point which inflicted heavy casualties on the Manchesters on 2 April and which the British Army called 'Manchester Hill'. The road running west from St. Quentin to Savy marked the southern end of the battlefield. A railway line from St. Quentin to Péronne crossed this road close to 'Manchester Quarry', its disused bed still clearly visible, marked 'Halte', and thence north-westwards across the fields.

On the morning of 1 April, the village of Savy was captured by troops of 97th Brigade. Later in the day the 15th and 16th Lancashire Fusiliers (96th Brigade) took over the advance and attacked north-eastwards, across an open and gently rising slope. The St. Quentin - Péronne railway line, raised on an embankment some 10-12 feet high, ran across the field in front of them, with a steeper slope beyond to a small hill known to the army as Round Hill, with Manchester Quarry lying immediately to the east. The casualties were heavy, but by mid-afternoon the Lancashire Fusiliers had reached the railway line cutting across their field of advance, and by the end of the day the 'Halte' was also taken. It was now the turn of the 2nd Manchesters to take over.

Major Lumsden

Lt. Col. Elstob

Wilfred Owen spent a month in this area, and as much of what he experienced here had a crucial influence on his later writing, it is well worth spending some time exploring it. In addition to April 1917, when Owen was here, the battlefield was the scene of stirring events in August 1914 and March 1918. Within less than a year and a space of a few hundred yards, two men - Major Lumsden in 1917 and Lieutenant-Colonel Elstob in 1918 - won the Victoria Cross in actions near the village of Francilly-Selency, the objective of the 2nd Manchesters on 2 April 1917.

At dawn that day the 2nd Manchesters advanced from the railway embankment across the battlefield, striking northwards in the direction of Holnon, with the village of Francilly-Selency as their objective. It lay to the right of the German strong point at Round Hill. The nearby hillock which came to be known after its capture by the 2nd Manchesters as Manchester Hill (together with the adjacent Quarry) was close to the railway junction, the 'Halte', but not easily visible from Round Hill. Both of these commanding positions were very strongly held, and the Manchesters suffered heavy additional casualties from six German 77 mm guns close to Francilly-Selency. The guns were finally captured by the Manchesters after bitter hand-to-hand fighting (Major Lumsden, Royal Marine Artillery, won a well-earned Victoria Cross for his part in recovering them the next day). Francilly-Selency was finally seized from the enemy forces, and the exhausted Manchesters consolidated their position just short of the main N.29 Holnon-St.Quentin road.

Visit: A good place to start the tour of this area is on the N 29 just east of Vermand, a village some three miles from the St Quentin motorway exit on the Amiens road. Take the D 73 and follow the road as far as Villevêque. Just through the village, turn on to the D 733 for Etreillers. It was in the fields to the right of this road that Owen investigated a German Albatross fighter which crashed on 8 April 1917, and removed some souvenirs from the wreck. Beyond the fields and looking half-right, the village of Beauvois is visible; this is where Owen joined the 2nd Manchesters at their HQ on 3 April 1917 before going on to the front line near Savy Wood. At Etreillers, continue through the village on the D 33 to a cross-roads; turn left on the D 32 towards Roupy.

Almost immediately on the right of the road is the Château de Pommery. Now a retirement home, on 2 April 1917 this was where the 2nd Manchesters formed up ready to depart for their attack on Francilly-Selency. It was here, too, that in March 1918 a sister battalion, the 17th Manchesters, fought in the château grounds as the garrison of what was then called Goodman Redoubt.

On 2 April 1917 the 2nd Manchesters crossed the fields to the left of the D 32, on their way towards Savy (which is visible in the distance) and the start line for their attack. Somewhere near here is the spot where Owen's friend Gaukroger was killed as they advanced - he was first buried in Roupy village, before being moved to Savy British Cemetery. As you reach Roupy cross-roads, turn left towards St. Quentin on to the busy D 930, and look to the left for the site of another redoubt in the chain of 1918 defences; this one, called Stanley Redoubt, was manned by the 19th battalion the King's Liverpools on 22 March 1918. In the first month of the war, on 27 August 1914, British troops, including Major Tom Bridges and his Dragoon Guards, passed through Roupy on their retreat from Mons.

About 400 yards from the cross-roads, turn left off the St. Quentin road into Roupy itself, and follow this small road past the church to a sharp right-hand bend beyond the village. The communal cemetery beside the road contains a number of British casualties from the fighting here. Holding a line of trench just behind the cemetery on 22 March 1918, a platoon of the 19th King's Liverpools made a desperate but vain attempt to stop the advancing Germans before they were overwhelmed and the few survivors captured. Continue along this road to the village of Savy. Just before it, the Savy British Cemetery on the left of the road holds some 800 graves. It is here that Owen's friend Gaukroger is

The Hindenburg Line.

British troops in Holnon Wood, close to Savy, Francilly-Selency and Manchester Hill.

buried, and also the only other officer of the 2nd Manchesters killed on the same day, 2 April 1917 - Second Lieutenant Winch of the Army Cyclist Corps (attached 2nd Manchesters).

Leave the cemetery and continue to a T-junction in Savy, turn right and almost immediately left to another T-junction (ignoring a right turn before it). Turn right here on to the D 681, a small straight road leading out of the village to Holnon. On 1 April 1917, the trench line located on the edge of the village here had been reached by the 11th (Lonsdale) Battalion of the Border Regiment, which had been given the task of capturing the village. It was also the start line for the next phase of the advance undertaken by two battalions of the Lancashire Fusiliers.

Continue along the Holnon road, the D 681. It was in the fields to the right of the road that the 15th and 16th battalions of the Lancashire Fusiliers suffered such heavy casualties on 1 April 1917 as they advanced to capture the railway line across the battlefield immediately in front of them, connecting St. Quentin with Vermand via the junction called 'The Halte'. The remains of the railway line and its embankment can be seen when stopping at the very prominent gas installation on the right of the road, about half a mile from Savy. It is marked on the map as 'Poste Gaz'.

Walk: Leave the car and walk eastwards along the former permanent way towards the woods, with St. Quentin beyond. It was in the railway embankment here that Wilfred Owen was nearly killed when a shell dropped close by, and in the wood immediately ahead that he lay in a hole close to what he thought were the remains of his friend Gaukroger. If you look to the right you can gain some idea of the formidable task that faced the Lancashire Fusiliers when they attacked across the fields on 1 April. [Owen's letters between 9 April and 14 May and his poem 'The Show' refer to this action.]

Visit: Return to the car at the 'Poste Gaz' and continue towards Holnon, still on the D 681. At the crossroads in Holnon, turn sharp right and continue to Francilly-Selency. At the cross-roads here, turn right on to the D 683 and into the village. Stop by the Mairie, to look at the memorial to the Manchesters - 2nd and 16th

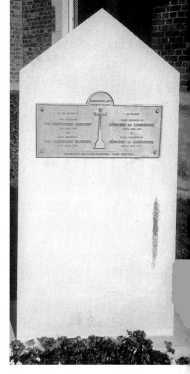

The Manchester Regiment memorial, Francilly-Selency, unveiled in 1996.

battalions - who fought here in 1917 and 1918 respectively. The Manchesters' capture of the German gun battery was achieved in the fields a few hundred yards away opposite the Mairie, and it was the recovery of these guns that gained Major Lumsden, R.M. Artillery, the Victoria Cross. The British memorial, inaugurated in 1996, stands close to the French village war memorial to their 1914-18 victims and another to the men who fought near here in the 1870 Franco-Prussian war.

Continue south along the D 683. A clump of trees, which comes into view almost immediately on the right of the road, marks the remains of Manchester Redoubt (usually called Manchester Hill), part of the defence line of redoubts set up in 1918. It was here that Lieutenant-Colonel Wilfrith Elstob won his Victoria Cross - but lost his life - on 21 March 1918. He has no known grave, but was buried by the Germans and must lie somewhere close to the Redoubt. If you turn right at the T junction on to the D 68 and stop at the first farm, it is possible to take a much closer look at the former redoubt.

Walk: If crops permit, it is worth walking along the side of the line of trees, then bearing to the right and going forward to a wooden post which is (usually) crowned with a rubber tyre. This marks the former observation post of the redoubt.

Drive on again southwards along the D 68, to reach 'The Halte' almost immediately. Although the railway track has long since been removed, the remains of its route across the road and the nearby railway station are clearly visible. Enemy fire from here held up the Fusiliers' advance. Taking the field path to the right, across the road from 'The Halte' and on for about 250 yards, brings you to a spot which reveals the task of the Lancashire Fusiliers and the Manchesters in their ultimate attempt to take Francilly-Selency.

Next day, 3 April, as they were recovering and counting the cost of this hard day's fighting, Second Lieutenant Wilfred Owen arrived to rejoin his unit, fresh and rested from the CCS and just in time to hear about his battalion's activities: no doubt there were jocular and/or caustic remarks on his talent at arriving just too late to take part. Here it was that Owen heard about the death in action of his friend Second Lieutenant Gaukroger, killed the previous day during the initial stages of the attack and initially buried at Roupy, the next village south of Savy.

Second Lieutenant Hubert Gaukroger: Owen recalled that he was known as 'Cock Robin'. Commissioned into the 1st Bn. Manchester Regiment, he left Marseilles with them on 8 December 1915 en route for Mesopotamia and reached Basra on 8 January 1916. Later attached to the 2nd Bn, he was 31 when killed in action on 2 April 1917 at Roupy while they were forming up for the attack on Francilly-Selency. He was buried in Savy. Owen identifed Gaukroger as the officer whose body lay buried nearby when Owen was in Savy Wood - but Gaukroger was killed and buried some distance away. The only other 2nd Manchesters' officer killed that day was Second Lieutenant H. W. Winch, of the Army Cyclist Corps: perhaps he was the officer referred to in Owen's letter home of 8 May (see below).

A divisional chaplain's diary for 4 April 1917 states that it snowed all day, with quite heavy falls. A group of men who had been kept in

The village of Savy, seen from the Roupy road.

BRITISH CEMETERY

Contemporary view of St Quentin during the occupation: German military band in the Grande Place. *(Paul Seret)*

reserve during the 2nd Manchesters' attack was sent forward to hold the front line on this date, including Wilfred Owen and his friend Captain Sorrel, who were replacements for casualties. As Owen wrote home shortly after, from Beauvois:

> *We stuck to our line 4 days (and 4 nights) without relief in the open, and in the snow... I never went off to sleep for those days because the others were far more fagged after several days of fighting than I, fresh from bed. We lay in wet snow. I kept alive on brandy, the fear of death, and the glorious prospect of the cathedral Town* [i.e. St. Quentin] *just below us, glittering with the morning.* [8 April 1917]

He also wrote to his young brother Colin about an incident on 8 April, Easter Sunday, when a French observation balloon cruising near St. Quentin was set on fire by a German fighter plane. The balloon's observer took to his parachute and the German plane, pursued and shot down by two French fighters, crashed in a field between Beauvois and Villevèque. Owen heard the noise and left his cellar billet:

> *I rushed up just in time to see a German Aeroplane come shuddering down from the sky ... The Machine was a new Albatross No. 2234. The Pilot – well I need not horrify you without need. But I took his handkerchief – a rather touching souvenir. You need not show them at home the spatter of blood in*

the corner. I rather want this handkerchief kept for me. The 3-ply wood is a bit of the body (of the machine).

He had other souvenirs for Colin too, from the quantity of clothing they found:

I took a Name Patch out of a Coat for you, and a Mark Note, which is specially interesting by reason of its date. 12 August 1914. It looks as if the plant for issuing these war notes was ready before the Declaration of War. [9 April 1917]

This chatty and observant letter was followed by an unusually long gap of more than two weeks, a period which was of the greatest significance in Owen's life, his writing and his ultimate fame.

The battalion's rest period in Beauvois ended on 14 April, when they were required to assist the French in an attack on the German front line trenches outside St. Quentin. Their particular objective was a short section of the German defensive system known as Dancour Trench; it lay north-west of the city, parallel with the D.732 road to Gricourt. The 2nd Manchesters' part in the venture was to start their attack from Bois des Roses, a small wood north-east of Francilly-Selency and south of the village of Fayet. Lieutenant-Colonel Noel Luxmoore, the CO, quickly realised that the direct route to this assembly point, leading over a prominent hill crest, would bring the battalion into a direct line of devastating fire from St. Quentin: the German defensive system of the Hindenburg Line would have a fine view of the troops before they even reached their official starting point.

After setting off at dawn on 14 April they therefore stopped short of the Bois des Roses hill top and looped back round to the west of Selency - presumably following the line of the old Roman road which still exists as a field track on the modern map - before bearing north across the main N.29 Amiens - St. Quentin road. Across the flat fields, the lie of the land on their right kept them out of enemy view, and a sunken road led them down as they swung round, heading south-east now, into the village of Fayet. A moment's alarm, and orders to 'line the road!' arose from nothing more threatening than a single German soldier running down the road towards them - to become the battalion's only prisoner that day.

Modern view of the Cathedral from the Dancour Trench area.

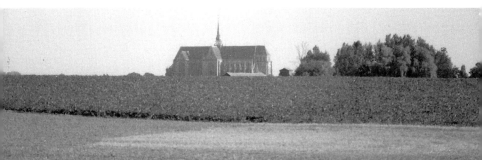

Squash Valley today. Crossing the ridge to the left, Owen's men were exposed to machine-gun fire: see 'Spring Offensive'.

The road still drops down between banks on the approach to Fayet from Gricourt, although it now has the additional feature of a motorway bridge over it. On the edge of the village the 2nd Manchesters branched off to the right and halted in a dip known to the British troops as 'Squash Valley'. Their next manoeuvre would take them up onto a narrow ridge, down the other side and into a copse ('Fig Wood') before assembling for the final attack. It was clear that as they reached the top of the ridge they would be exposed to the enemy defences on the edge of St. Quentin; the pause in Squash Valley was a final moment of peace. Shortly after mid-day the battalion left the safety of the valley, crossed the ridge and dropped down on its eastern side and through Fig Wood to the shelter of the assembly point south of Fayet village.

As foreseen, the Germans placed heavy calibre artillery fire on the troops as soon as they came into view on the crest of the hill, until they were safely out of sight once more at the bottom. From here it was clear that the attack on the trench involved climbing up a fairly steep valley slope, with a turn of almost 90 degrees at the top to achieve a frontal approach to Dancour Trench. In order to protect the right flank of the Manchesters during their attack on the trench, the 1st Battalion Dorsetshire Regiment had by 9 am captured Cepy Farm near it and extended their battalion line south-westward to run parallel to the direction of Manchesters' forthcoming attack. The attack on Cepy Farm was not without casualties, for the small German garrison continued to fire until the British were within 50 yards of the farm when they fled.

Contemporary view of St Quentin Cathedral from Cepy road, close to Dancour Trench.

The attack was led by A Company with Owen at the head of his section. As they charged up the slope and turned right to the German trench, rifle fire caught them from behind, on the edge of Fayet - fortunately dealt with promptly by the following troops. It seems to have been something of an anticlimax when they reached the trench, for they found it empty. They explored the defences, and returned to Savy.

The day's events found their way into a letter to his mother, and another to his brother Colin. To Susan, Wilfred wrote:

Our A Company led the Attack and of course lost a certain number of men. [30 were killed] *I had some extraordinary escapes from shells & bullets ...Never before has the Battalion encountered such intense shelling as rained on us as we advanced in the open. The Colonel sent round this message the next day: 'I was filled with admiration at the conduct of the Battalion under the heavy shell-fire ... The leadership of officers was excellent, and the conduct of the men beyond praise.'* [25 April 1917]

Three weeks later, to Colin, he described what it felt like:

The sensations of going over the top are about as exhilarating as those dreams of falling over a precipice, when you see the rocks at the bottom surging up to you. I woke up without being squashed. Some didn't. There was an extraordinary exultation in the act of slowly walking forward, showing ourselves openly. ... There was no bugle and no drum for which I was very sorry. I kept up a kind of chanting sing-song:

58

Keep the Line straight! Not so fast on the left! Steady on the Left!
Not so fast! Then we were caught up in a Tornado of Shells. The
various 'waves' were all broken up and we carried on like a
crowd moving off a cricket-field. When I looked back and saw the
ground all crawling and wormy with wounded bodies, I felt no
horror at all but only an immense exultation at having got
through the Barrage. [14 May 1917]

More than a year later, when Owen was in Scarborough in July 1918
and then on his return to France the following month, he wrote 'Spring
Offensive', much of which can be related to the surroundings and
events of this day: in the valley,

> *Halted against the shade of a last hill*
> *They fed, and eased of pack-loads, were at ease;*
> *And leaning on the nearest chest or knees*
> *Carelessly slept. But many there stood still*
> *To face the stark blank sky beyond the ridge,*
> *Knowing their feet had come to the end of the world.*

The description a few lines later of how 'the buttercups/had blessed
with gold their slow boots coming up' echoes a childhood memory of
buttercup petals clinging to his boots on a river-meadow walk. The
poem moves sharply into his adult wartime experience as the men
reach the top of the ridge between Squash Valley and Fig Wood:

> *So, soon they topped the hill, and raced together*
> *Over an open stretch of herb and heather*

Artist's impression of a British advance towards German lines.

> *Exposed. And instantly the whole sky burned*
> *With fury against them ...*

Before that, however, the image from his letter to Colin of the ground 'all crawling and wormy with wounded bodies' had found its way into his poetry: 'The Show', first drafted in November 1917, has powerful images of 'thin caterpillars' which 'writhed and shrivelled, killed' in a land that was 'grey, cratered like the moon with hollow woe'. (This also recalls an earlier letter to Susan Owen, about the battlefield round Munich Trench in January 1917, as a

> *'body of foulest disease and its odour is the breath of cancer*
> *...No Man's Land under snow is like the face of the moon chaotic,*
> *crater-ridden, uninhabitable, awful, the abode of madness'* [19
> January 1917])

After this attack, the 2nd Manchesters spent some days in Savy Wood. Here, as Wilfred remarks in a letter, their reward for their efforts around Fayet was:

> *... to remain in the Line 12 days. For twelve days I did not*
> *wash my face, nor take off my boots nor sleep a deep sleep. For*
> *twelve days we lay in holes ...*[25 April 1917]

One incident, when they were lying up against a railway embankment, seems to have burdened Owen with unmanageable stress:

> *A big shell lit on the top of the bank, just 2 yards from my*
> *head. Before I awoke, I was blown in the air right away from the*
> *bank! I passed most of the following days in a railway Cutting,*
> *in a hole just big enough to lie in, and covered with corrugated*
> *iron. My brother officer of B Coy, 2/Lt Gaukroger lay opposite in*
> *a similar hole. But he was covered with earth, and no relief will*
> *ever relieve him, nor will his Rest be a 9 days-Rest.* [25 April
> 1917]

His next letter, dated 2 May, came from the 13th Casualty Clearing Station: Lieutenant-Colonel Noel Luxmoore, his Commanding

Savy British cemetery, the location of Gaukroger's grave.

Officer, had observed that he was shaky, his memory impaired, and that he was in no fit state to lead his men. Second Lieutenant Owen was withdrawn from the line and despatched to the Casualty Clearing Station that he had left only a month earlier, at Gailly on the Somme canal.

Visit to the Fayet area: approaching St. Quentin on the N.29 road, go past the right turn to Holnon and take the next turn on the left - a small road only 300 yards further on, running along the side of a small copse. As the road bends slightly to the right, note some waste building material on the left: this was the Enghien Redoubt, another of the 1918 line of strong-points, garrisoned at the time by a detachment of the Ox. & Bucks. Light Infantry. Continue over the bridge spanning the motorway and descend into the village of Fayet. At the junction at the bottom coming down from the bridge, take a very sharp turn to the right, along a minor residential road rather than the 90-degree right turn up to the village centre. The field facing you at the end of this short road is where the Manchesters rested before continuing to their assembly position, and which they called Squash Valley. Turn up to the left, and at the top of the rise turn right along the crest of the ridge through a small housing estate. Stop the car at the end. Squash Valley is on your right, and Fig Wood is the small copse beyond the field on your left. The Manchesters came over the crest where the houses now stand and descended through the wood to what is now a busy shopping and commercial centre. (This is the place to read Owen's letters of 25 April and 14 May, describing the day's events, and also 'Spring Offensive'.)

Reverse direction and turn right, out of the housing estate and on to the D.57, with the shopping centre quickly visible on the right, where the Manchesters formed up for their attack. Look up to the left: this is the valley up which they made their attack. Continue for a short distance and turn left into the Rue de Lille, follow it to the T-junction at the end and turn left on to the D.732. Continue for a few hundred yards and stop on the wide verge at the right hand side of the road.

This was the site of Dancour Trench, the 2nd Manchesters' objective which they gained and explored on 14 April 1917. Down to the left across the road, their assembly point in the shopping centre at the bottom of the valley is clearly visible. The reason for the siting of the forward defence here, and the challenge of approaching it, are easily appreciated.

Notes and Sources

A Deep Cry, ed. Anne Powell, pub. Palladour Books 1993
The History of The Lancashire Fusiliers 1914-1918, J. C. Latter, Gale & Polden, 1949
The History of The Manchester Regiment, H.C.Wylly, Vol.2, Foster Groom & Co. Ltd., 1925
History of the 15th Bn. The Highland Light Infantry, T. Chalmers, McCallum & Co., Glasgow 1934
History of the 16th Bn The Highland Light Infantry, T. Chalmers, McCallum & Co., Glasgow, 1930

Two war-time views of the Somme canal east of Gailly, showing the meanders of the river, trenches and shell holes.

Chapter Three

'A DAMNED FINE POET'

(Robert Graves, December 1917)

By this time the CCS at Gailly, which Owen already knew from his previous treatment for concussion, was designated specifically for 'neurasthenia' cases. This would seem to indicate a rather depressing atmosphere, with patients showing no physical wounds, which in many cases could create supportive and friendly relationships, but only men who needed to rest and retrieve their emotional and mental stability. However, Owen seemed very relieved and pleased to be there and, writing the day after his arrival, he asserted stoutly that his family should 'not for a moment suppose I have had a 'breakdown'. I am simply avoiding one' (2 May 1917), repeating the point a week later.

As his arrival at Gailly was registered, he was delighted to find an old school-friend entering his name and age - 'old Hartop of the Technical': an unexpected bonus and reminder of earlier days in Shrewsbury. The obvious and unusual fraternity between Owen-the-officer and Hartop-the-Other-Rank startled soldiers standing around.

Owen's Shrewsbury friends and the war. Hartop, a married man who like Owen had joined up in 1915, was now Store Corporal at the CCS, an evidently undemanding role. Unlike Owen, however, he survived the war and returned to Shrewsbury and a teaching career. Others among Owen's group of pre-war Shrewsbury friends were less fortunate: 'Bill' Bulman, whose mother was a close friend of Susan

Gailly, Cerisy and the Somme canal.

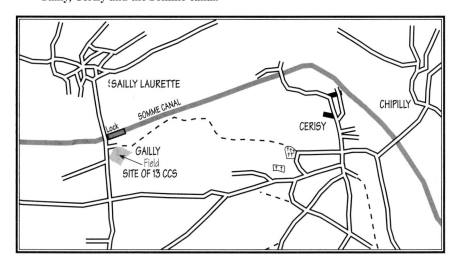

The lock at Gailly on the side of which is an engraved stone commemorating the Royal Engineers' reconstruction work in October 1918. The Owen plinth was inaugurated in June 1998 by the local community.

Owen (and whom the Owen family had visited in Scotland for a family holiday in 1912), was killed in July 1915 whilst in action in Gallipoli with the 4th Battalion King's Own Scottish Borderers. Major Walter Forrest, of the same battalion and who was engaged to Bill Bulman's sister Blanche, was killed in Palestine in April 1917. Stanley Webb, who like Hartop had joined the RAMC, was later commissioned and wounded at Monchy le Preux, and was killed in action during the retreat of March 1918 while serving with the 9th East Surreys. Another loss in 1918 was that of John Ragge, whose home was next to the Owen family house, 'Mahim', in Monkmoor Road, Shrewsbury. Ragge, son of an Inland Revenue employee, joined the 15th London Regiment (Civil Service Rifles). After recovering from a wound he was posted to the 8th Battalion, Gloucestershire Regiment, and was killed in an attack at the Boars Head trenches at Neuve Chapelle in September 1918. He has no known grave, and his name is recorded on the Loos Memorial.

The German retreat to the Hindenburg Line meant that some of the Casualty Clearing Stations in the Somme area were too far behind the front line to be convenient, and the Director of Medical Services issued new orders. No. 21 CCS at Corbie was to close, its remaining patients, mostly 'shell-shock' and self-inflicted wound cases, were to be sent to the CCS at Gailly, and Captain W. Brown RAMC(T), a neurologist at the Corbie CCS, was to go with them. Although Owen had not been physically wounded, his experiences at Serre and now in the attacks on the Hindenburg Line had left their mark mentally, and with the arrival of Dr Brown he came under the care of a specialist in neurasthenia. The reconstituted unit at Gailly became No. 41 Stationary Hospital, and for a month after his arrival Owen was treated here. On 7 June 1917 he moved to No. 1 General Hospital at Etretat on the coast, and eventually arrived at the Welsh Hospital at Netley, Southampton.

Little is known of how this particular young officer was treated for 'neurasthenia', popularly known as 'shell-shock' - and essentially the same condition as that known to the late twentieth century as 'Post Traumatic Stress Disorder' or 'PTSD'. The standard treatment for this distressing affliction was plenty of rest and quiet; the great majority of men affected during the First World War were given a period of complete rest, well away from the front line but still clearly within the military zone, and the physical recuperation usually enabled them to be returned to active military life within two or three weeks. The number returned to England was small.

While he was at Gailly, Owen had time to write long letters home, and remarked (4 May) that 'nothing happens; only a great calm happiness. We are a cheery crowd here this time'. In a letter to his sister (8 May) he comments that 'everyone I meet knows someone that I know' and 'I am .. so indolent and well-looked after.' In the same letter, however, he referred to the reason for his presence in the hospital:

> ... it was not the Bosche that worked me up, nor the explosives, but it was living so long by poor old Cock Robin (as we used to call 2/Lt. Gaukroger), who lay not only near by, but in various places around and about ...

As indicated above, this seems to indicate confusion on Owen's part.

He also used the time to read, to explore the countryside, and even to hitch a ride on the canal on a fine hot day, enjoying the scenery gliding past and dreaming of past ages - an experience that inspired his poem 'Hospital Barge at Cérisy', written in December 1917 when he was in Scarborough. Although it dates from his most creative period, with the war present in many poems, 'Hospital Barge' is a reflection of the dreamy summer heat, with thoughts of King Arthur, Merlin and Avalon filling the calm scene. His letter referring to the expedition reflects the peace of the day and the scene.

Walk: There is an easy and very pleasant walk of about 1.5 km along the canal bank between Gailly and Cerisy. From the main Amiens - St. Quentin road, turn north at Lamotte-Warfusée and park beside the canal lock at Gailly. The tow-path is kept clear along the southern bank of the canal, which runs in a straight line here as far as Cerisy. To approach this stretch from the other end, take the minor road down to Cerisy from the main road and follow signs to the 'stade', the village sports ground. Park outside the sports ground; the canal bank is accessible beside the narrow bridge leading across the canal to a group of holiday cabins and caravans (this is a very popular fishing area).

A few days later, a letter to his young brother Colin (now nearly 17), reflected a more war-like approach to life. He described 'some Loot' from the crashed German plane which he obtained with Colin in mind (including a bugle which he later decided to keep). In vivid style he describes the action at Fayet, quoted above; and then continues, first into discussion of what Colin might do after the war, and thence into a lengthy Biblical fantasy. This continues in the next letter to his mother two days later, in which he discusses his attitude to Christianity and its message of avoiding killing. This contains a phrase which has been much quoted: 'And am I not myself a conscientious objector with a very seared conscience?' and continues,

Christ is literally in no man's land. There men often hear His voice: Greater love hath no man than this, that a man lay down his life - for a friend.... Thus you see how pure Christianity will not fit in with pure patriotism. [16 May 1917]

Back in England once more, Owen attended a Medical Board at Netley on 25 June 1917, presided over by Lieutenant-Colonel H. Cook RAMC, the CO of the hospital. The Board's report begins:

The Board find that in March 1917, 2nd Lt. W. E. S. Owen of the 5th (attached 2nd) Bn. Manchester Regiment, fell down a well at Bouchoir and was momentarily stunned. He was under Medical Treatment for 3 weeks and then resumed duty. About the middle of April he was blown up by a shell explosion while asleep. On May 1st he was observed to be shaky and tremulous and his conduct and manner were peculiar and his memory confused. The R.M.O. sent him to No. 41 Stationary Hospital Gailly where he was under observation and treatment by

Captain Brown RAMC, neurological specialist, for a month. On 7.6.17 he was transferred to the Welsh hospital Netley. There is little abnormality to be observed but he seems to be of a highly strung temperament. He has slept well while here. He leaves hospital today transferred to Craiglockhart War Hospital Edinburgh for special observation and treatment.

The Owen family had visited Scotland on family holidays, and in his teenage years Wilfred had enjoyed exploring Edinburgh, Walter Scott's territory and the battle ground of Flodden Field. Now, however, he reached the northern capital on a different mission and on 26 June he wrote home from Craiglockhart War Hospital, Slateford, near the southern edge of the city. His overnight journey north brought him into the city in time to 'breakfast hugely' before walking 'the lovely length of Princes Street. The Castle looked more than ever a Hallucination, with the morning sun behind it.'

Craiglockhart: the main building, formerly a spa hotel, remains very much the same outside as when Owen knew it. In 'Memoirs of an Infantry Officer', Siegfried Sassoon described it as a crowded establishment, cheerful by day but gloomy by night when men lay awake in desperation, trying to avoid the nightmares of shell-shock. Sassoon was treated by the famous Dr. William Rivers, an anthropologist and neurologist who was the Chief Medical Officer. After the war Craiglockhart became a teacher-training establishment and in due course the headquarters of Napier University. In sharp contrast to its atmosphere in 1917, it is now a busy and cheerful building with students' refectories named after Sassoon and Owen.

Craiglockhart, Edinburgh: from psychiatric hospital in 1917 to Napier University.

Owen was treated by Dr. Brock, who favoured the 'occupation cure': sufferers from neurasthenia should be encouraged to be active and to follow their own interests and instincts. Wilfred was directed into botany - he addressed the establishment on the subject of 'Do Plants Think?' - into teaching (following his experience in Shrewsbury as a pupil-teacher and in France as an English teacher and private tutor) - and, because of his enthusiasm for language and writing, into being the editor of the house magazine, The Hydra. The war hospital had its network of

Captain Rivers   *Major Ruggles*   *Captain Brock*

'Our M.O's' – Craiglockhart's three medical officers, as pictured in the house magazine *The Hydra*.

supporters who visited patients or invited them out, and the city itself provided distraction and interest. The best medicine of all, it seemed to Wilfred, was a visit from his mother.

Writing for *The Hydra* - articles and reviews as well as editorials - was a happy occupation, and in August his literary interests received immense encouragement from an unexpected source: he met Siegfried Sassoon. Sassoon, who had enlisted as a trooper in the Sussex Yeomanry in 1914, was a lieutenant in the Royal Welch Fusiliers - and also a published and unusual poet. He arrived at Craiglockhart in July 1917 designated as suffering from shell-shock, a few days before the publication of his famous protest against the management of the war, for which he originally hoped to be court-martialled; but his acknowledged courage - he had won the Military Cross for rescuing wounded men near Fricourt in May 1916 - made this difficult for the British Army authorities. He was sent into Rivers' care, and was initially inclined to be dismissive of the rather diffident Wilfred Owen.

An aspiring romantic and pastoral poet before the war, Sassoon was gaining an unexpected reputation for his war poetry, unrepentantly forthright about the dangers, the misery, the gaps in perception between the front line and the rear, and also the warmth and comradeship to be found in the trenches. Bored by his life at Craiglockhart, he took an interest in Owen, came to recognise his talents - and encouraged him to use his war experiences in his writing.

This chance encounter, which grew into a friendship of the greatest importance to Owen, came at a crucial moment. The body of work for which Owen became - and remains - famous dates almost entirely from the period beginning in August 1917, when he met Sassoon, until his death early in November 1918: an astonishing burst of creativity written in apparently unpromising circumstances. Probably the most famous of Owen's poems to come out of this new creativity was 'Anthem for Doomed Youth' ('What passing bells for these who die as cattle ...'), to which Sassoon made a few alterations and suggested 'Anthem' for the title.

Both then and later, Sassoon also introduced Owen to other writers and patrons - Robert Graves, H. G. Wells, Arnold Bennett, Robert Ross - and steered him into the type of life which he would probably have adopted permanently if he had survived the war. Graves corresponded with him in the autumn of 1917, commenting in detail on the structure and rhythm of his poetry and ideas, and urging him on to further efforts.

A fortnight after his first meeting with Sassoon, Owen wrote to his mother that, 'I still have disastrous dreams, but they are taking on a more civilian character, motor accidents and so on' [2 September 1917], but by the end of October he had been passed fit by a Medical Board and reported to the 5th (Reserve) Bn Manchester Regiment, in Scarborough. Whether it was the activity, the friendship with Sassoon or the poetry writing - or simply the passage of time away from the war - that achieved the cure, cannot be judged. Since he left them ten months earlier to join the 2nd Manchesters on active service in France, the 5th Manchesters had relocated from Southport to Ripon and then to Burniston Camp on the edge of Scarborough. (The barracks area has now been built over, although a small section of the camp and the parade ground can still be identified.) Assigned by the Medical Board to 'light duties', Wilfred Owen now became responsible for domestic routine in the officers' quarters, not in the barracks but in the Clarence Gardens Hotel (now the Clifton Hotel) overlooking the North Bay, Scarborough. He received a warm welcome from all ranks of the 5th Manchesters, who had been under the impression that he had been killed. Now, as he wrote, 'I had risen from the dead'.

The Commanding Officer was a regular soldier, Lieutenant-Colonel Mitchell, who was inclined to bad temper in the mornings - Owen, whose Mess Secretary duties included seeing that the Colonel's bathwater was hot when required, recorded him as holding an 'Orderly Room' on Christmas Day and awarding punishments 'right and left and above and below' in direct contravention of King's Regulations. Men passed through Scarborough on their way to their next posting overseas, and large overseas drafts created plenty of clerical work; Owen escaped from this, and from the officers' endless games of bridge, into his turret bedroom where he wrote and drafted the poems that were growing in his consciousness. This was where the first of his poems to be published, 'Miners', developed out of a vision glimpsed in glowing coal that evoked not only the creation of coal itself in the remote past but the bodies of miners who had died crushed in mines - and also the bodies of men killed in mines at war. It was inspired by a genuine mining accident reported in January 1918, formed rapidly in his mind, and appeared in *The Nation* on 26 January 1918.

By day, Owen's duties included the supervision of around seventy officers, including some who had been placed under open arrest - and to accompany officers under arrest on exercise along the cliff path. In the case of a subaltern (a former Sergeant-major) who was under arrest for striking the Assistant Provost Marshal, Owen remarked that he took care to keep on the landward side of the cliff. Newly commissioned officers were felt as a nuisance with constant pestering, and Owen, a senior subaltern who had

The Clifton Hotel, Scarborough, formerly the Clarence Gardens, the Officers' Mess where in 1917 Owen occupied one of the turret rooms.

View of Scarborough with Owen's hotel overlooking the North Bay.

seen active service, looked forward to his promotion to Lieutenant, due on 4 December 1917 and to the increase in pay from 10s 6d to 11s 6d per day, not knowing that the Military Secretary's office would fail to consult their records and that he would therefore continue to wear his Second Lieutenant's badges until he was killed.

At the end of 1917 he marked the turn of the year by reviewing the past twelve months and considering the future. In a long letter to his mother he reflected on his friendships, but mostly on himself, with vivid images of past and present (the 'dreadful encampment' referred to here was Etaples):

> *And so I have come to the true measure of man. I am not dissatisfied with my years ... I go out of this year a Poet, my dear Mother, as which I did not enter it. I am held peer by the Georgians; I am a poet's poet. I am started. The tugs have left me; I feel the great swelling of the open sea taking my galleon. Last year, at this time ... I lay awake in a windy tent in the middle of a vast, dreadful encampment. It seemed neither France nor England, but a kind of paddock where the beasts are kept a few days before the shambles. I heard the revelling of the Scotch troops, who are now dead, and who knew they would be dead. ...I thought of the very strange look on all faces in that camp ... It was not despair, or terror, it was more terrible than terror, for it was a blindfold look, and without expression, like a dead rabbit's. It will never be painted, and no actor will ever seize it. And to describe it, I think I must go back and be with them. [31 December 1917]*

Three weeks before this letter he wrote the poem 'Wild with all Regrets' (later expanded into 'A Terre') which expresses the thoughts and feelings of a war-disabled officer. His time at Scarborough had produced a number of poems in draft form as well as completed pieces such as 'Hospital Barge' and 'Miners' - the shell-shock had evidently gone and his creative mind was working well.

As with other officers in Scarborough originally classified as 'fit for light duties', Owen was in due course posted to Northern Command depot at Ripon. Before leaving he recorded a congenial dinner in Scarborough with a recent friend, Second Lieutenant Bainbrigge of the 5th Bn. Lancashire Fusiliers.

Philip Bainbrigge, a former schoolmaster (at Shrewsbury School, a pleasing coincidence for Owen) was also a poet and an amusing companion. He was well-known in the school for his elegant classical verse. Physically unsuited for military life

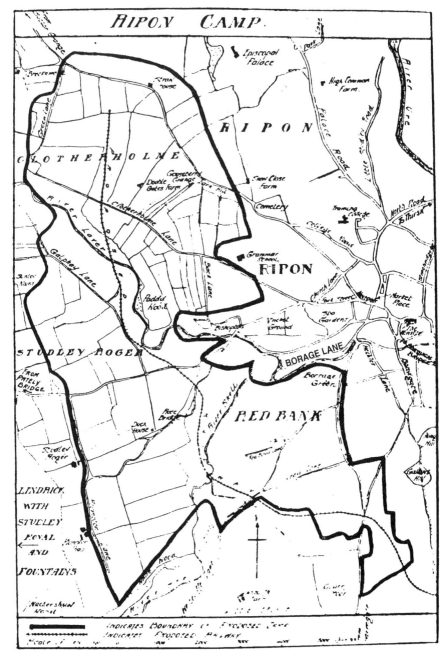

Ripon Camp in 1918, with Borage Lane on the route from camp to town centre.

(he was extremely short-sighted), he enlisted in the Lancashire Fusiliers after learning of the death in action of two schoolmaster colleagues, Malcolm White and Evelyn Southwell, and was himself killed in action at Ronssoy in September 1918 while attached to the 24th Battalion Welch Regiment. He is buried in Five Points Cemetery, Lechelle. At the inaugural ceremony for the school's memorial to its members of staff killed in the war, he was described as 'magnificently unsuited for war in everything except courage'.

Wilfred Owen arrived in Ripon on 12 March 1918, on the eve of an unexpected and dramatic change in the course of the war, the German breakthrough of 21 March. The move to Ripon was not a welcome change, for at first Owen found it 'An awful Camp - huts - dirty blankets', but he found a way of combining the demands of military life and his own need to write. As in London, when during his Artists Rifles training days he rented a room of his own, he now found a quiet cottage room in Borage Lane, a pleasant rural approach to the city from the training camp.

Ripon Cathedral.

The great camp was busily active, training squads of young conscripts and processing them along their route towards the front line, but once his day's drilling sessions ended at 3 pm, Owen escaped from his army identity and concentrated on his poetry. Remembering Sassoon's advice to write about his war experiences, and using the techniques learned at Craiglockhart, he drew on the events that had led to shell-shock, and during these spring months of 1918 drafted, wrote and re-wrote the poems which still show us some of the realities of war.

'The Send-Off' describes the departure of a freshly-trained squad by train, a group of conscripts prepared for war service but barely identifiable as individuals. The poet recognises that many of them will not return, and that though they sang as they set off, those few who survived would '.. creep back, silent, to village wells/Up half-known roads'. Other poems from this intensively fruitful period include 'Mental Cases', and possibly 'Strange Meeting'.

Awareness of the war pressed home on him. As he commented to his sister Mary during the sudden German advance in March 1918,

It is specially cruel for me to hear of all we gained by St.

73

The house (with skylight) in Borage Lane where Wilfred Owen rented a room in 1918 in order to write.

> *Quentin having been lost. They are dying again at Beaumont Hamel, which already in 1916 was cobbled with skulls.* [25 March 1918]

This striking phrase can be linked with 'Insensibility', a poem drafted in the winter of 1917-18 and probably revised in Ripon, which begins:

> *Happy are men who yet before they are killed*
> *Can let their veins run cold.*
> *Whom no compassion fleers*
> *Or makes their feet*
> *Sore on the alleys cobbled with their brothers.*

In April 1918, the anniversary of his joining the 2nd Manchesters at St. Quentin, he wrote to his cousin that he was haunted by the vision of the lands about St. Quentin 'crawling with wounded', an image that appears in his poem 'The Show' about his experiences there. Other place-names appeared in the news that were reminders of his months of active service - Gailly, the site of 13 CCS on the Somme canal, and Nesle, where he was delayed for three days at the end of March 1917, both now over-run.

By the beginning of June 1918 Owen was pronounced fit for Active Service. His father's remark at this news - 'Gratified to know you are normal again' - perhaps indicates Tom Owen's discomfiture at his son's shell-shock. Wilfred was posted back to the 5th Manchesters in Scarborough - to a tent inside the camp, this time, rather than in the comfort of a private turret room in the Clarence Gardens Hotel. Acting as battalion Messing Officer as well as training new young recruits, he commented on 'a special rumpus' at a War Office decree that those under the age of 19 were to have more bread and meat than their elders.

Despite his seniority (now more than two years) and his responsibilities, Owen was still a Second Lieutenant. In a letter to his mother from Scarborough dated 15 July 1918 he wrote, 'I still wear one pip because nobody knows whether I am a Lieutenant or not'. His promotion to full Lieutenant was finally promulgated on 5 November 1918, the day after his death; his father Tom Owen queried the promotion, which came to his notice in correspondence with the War Office in January 1919. Owen's contemporaries in the Artists Rifles, commissioned at the same time, all appear to have reached full lieutenant's rank after the usual period of eighteen months. No one, including Owen himself, seems to have tried to clarify his status.

By now, however, rank was not high on his list of considerations. Although a permanent home posting had been

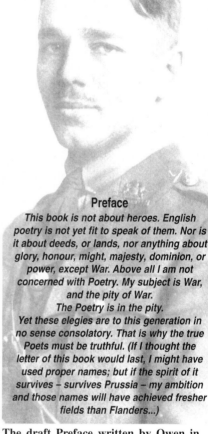

Preface
This book is not about heroes. English poetry is not yet fit to speak of them. Nor is it about deeds, or lands, nor anything about glory, honour, might, majesty, dominion, or power, except War. Above all I am not concerned with Poetry. My subject is War, and the pity of War.
The Poetry is in the pity.
Yet these elegies are to this generation in no sense consolatory. That is why the true Poets must be truthful. (If I thought the letter of this book would last, I might have used proper names; but if the spirit of it survives – survives Prussia – my ambition and those names will have achieved fresher fields than Flanders...)

The draft Preface written by Owen in Ripon for a collection of war poems that he hoped to publish in 1919.

discussed, with Sassoon and others in his literary circle hoping to ensure it, it seems unlikely that it could have been obtained; and Owen himself was by now determined to return to the front line. As he wrote to his mother that summer, 'I am much gladder to be going out again than afraid. I shall be better able to cry my outcry, playing my part.' [10 August 1918] He was very conscious of his self-allotted role, to speak out for the men whose front-line experiences could not be imagined by

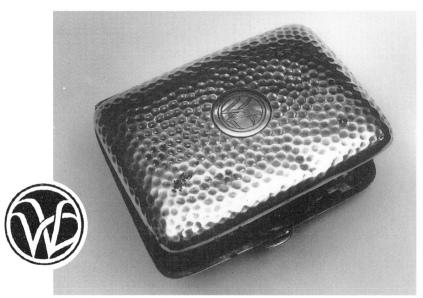

Owen's cigarette case with his monogram, using his initials W E S O, now used as the emblem of the Wilfred Owen Association.

the civilian at home, as he put it in 'The Calls', which ends:

I heard the sighs of men, that have no skill
To speak of their distress, no, nor the will!
A voice I know. And this time I must go.

In London that month Owen visited Sassoon in hospital, wounded in the head and weary, and wrote to him afterwards, 'I'm in hasty retreat towards the Front. Battle is easier here; and therefore you will stay and endure old men and women to the End, and wage the bitterer war and more hopeless.' [31 August 1918]

By the end of August 1918 Owen was on his way to France: he was not to see England again.

Chapter 3: Notes & Sources
PRO: WO 138/4
Stand To! Journal of the Western Front Association, No. 50, September 1997

Chapter Four

THE FRONT LINE AGAIN

As for so many thousands, the British base at Etaples was once again Owen's first stop in France, with its vast acres - street upon street of hutments and tents, hospitals, stores of every kind. Its notoriously aggressive and brutal atmosphere led to violent protests in September 1917, and thereafter the approach to training and discipline became somewhat more relaxed. Owen's first visit there, over New Year's Eve 1916-17, was extremely brief, but this second visit lasted a week and, as he reported in a postcard home, 'This place is vastly more habitable than in 1917. Impossible to feel depressed.' After enjoying some congenial companionship he was posted back to the 2nd Manchesters; the Staff at the Base indicated that they were doing it as a kindness, but it is more likely that it was because the Manchesters were in dire need of reinforcements - during the last few days of August the battalion had suffered five officer casualties, including two Company Commanders.

Owen departed in an officer draft to the Manchesters together with Major J. L. Murphy, a Company Commander replacement who eventually became Second in Command of the battalion, and Second Lieutenant John Foulkes who later, like Owen, won the Military Cross for gallantry during the attack on the Fonsomme Line at Joncourt.

By now the tide of war had turned and the 'last hundred days' to victory were sweeping away the German advances of recent months. Owen rejoined the 2nd Manchesters at La Neuville, outside Corbie and not far from the 13 CCS location at Gailly - but he had changed since then, and so had the battalion. Lieutenant-Colonel Luxmoore, who had noted Owen's strange behaviour at Savy Wood in April 1917, had departed to a Staff posting and the battalion was now commanded by Lieutenant-Colonel G. M. Robertson of the North Staffordshire Regiment. In his letter of 21 September, Owen remarked that 'The Colonel is an agreeable non-ferocious gentleman', but he says of the Second in Command that 'he loves Soldiering and has passed his life wherever he could find any fighting.' A few days later he expanded on this description:

Major Marshall of the 10 wounds is the most arrant utterly soldierly soldier I ever came across ... Bold, robust, dashing, unscrupulous, cruel, jovial, immoral, vast-chested, handsome-headed, of free, coarse speech ... [28 September 1918]

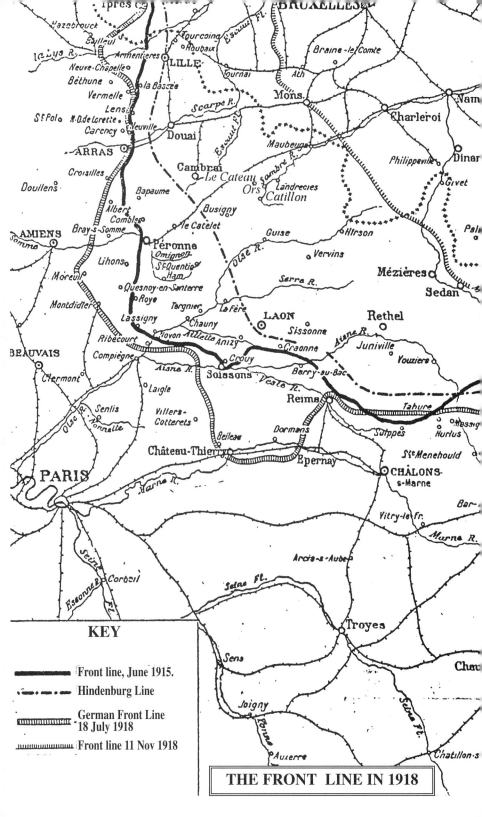

THE FRONT LINE IN 1918

KEY

Front line, June 1915.

Hindenburg Line

German Front Line 18 July 1918

Front line 11 Nov 1918

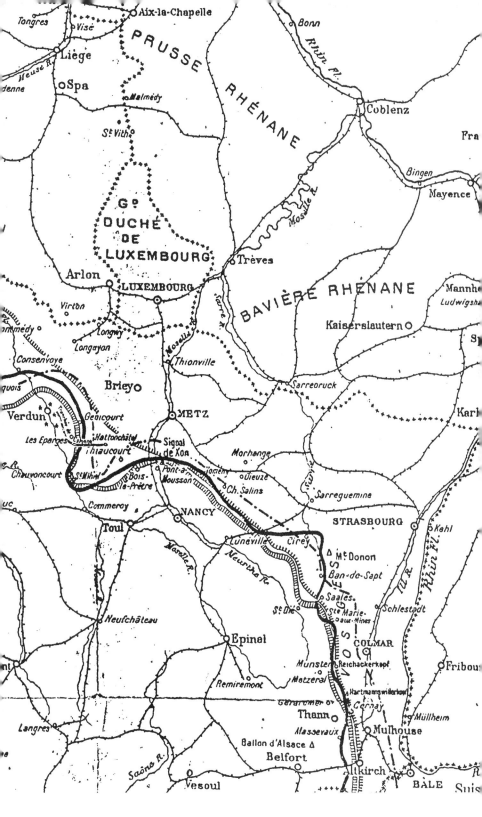

After working as a clerk in the Birmingham University Medical Faculty, John Marshall (born in 1887) became a vet in Essex and at the outbreak of war was employed by the War Office Remounts Department. This involved purchasing horses from the Argentine, and carried officer rank. During the war he was transferred to the Irish Guards, was wounded ten times and won the Military Cross and Bar (also the French Croix de Guerre and Belgian Chevalier of the Order of Leopold). Wilfred Owen seems to have been somewhat wary of his brusque manner: one of his letters refers to him as 'the Terrible Major'.

This was Lieutenant (Acting Major) J. N. Marshall, MC, Irish Guards, recently posted to the Manchesters and destined to win the Victoria Cross at Ors some two months hence.

The 2nd Manchesters were still in the 32nd Division but had now left the 14th Brigade and were serving alongside the 15th and 16th Lancashire Fusiliers, commanded by Lieutenant-Colonel Alban and Lieutenant-Colonel Stone, in the 96th Brigade. Owen was assigned to the 2nd Manchesters' D Company under Captain H. Somerville, M.C. and Bar; when Somerville was wounded in the attack at Joncourt at the beginning of October, Owen took his place. Writing home to his mother, he described their conditions:

... there is here all but all that a man wants fundamentally; letters from Home of good news, shelter from the rain and cold; an intellectual gentleman for Captain; 3 bright and merry boys for my corporals; & stout grizzled old soldiers in my platoon. My Sergeant is a tiny man. We get on very well together. ... The Colonel is a mild, honourable gentleman, who lets us alone to do our work. [28 September 1918]

His poetry was still vital to him, and these September days saw him revising a poem first drafted in Scarborough in July. This was 'Spring Offensive', a description of the action he had experienced around St. Quentin in April 1917. Describing first the slow steady approach to battle, and rest on a hot sunny hillside, it leaps into the 'fury' of enemy fire and recalls his advance over the hill-top at Fayet; the moments that he described in letters home soon after that day, of 'going over the top' [letter, 14 May 1917] end with reflection on the impossibility of explaining battle experience to those who have not lived through it: 'Why speak not they of comrades that went under?'

Another poem from this period was 'Smile, Smile, Smile', its title taken from one of the most popular British songs of the day ('What's the use of worrying?/It never was worth while/So pack up your

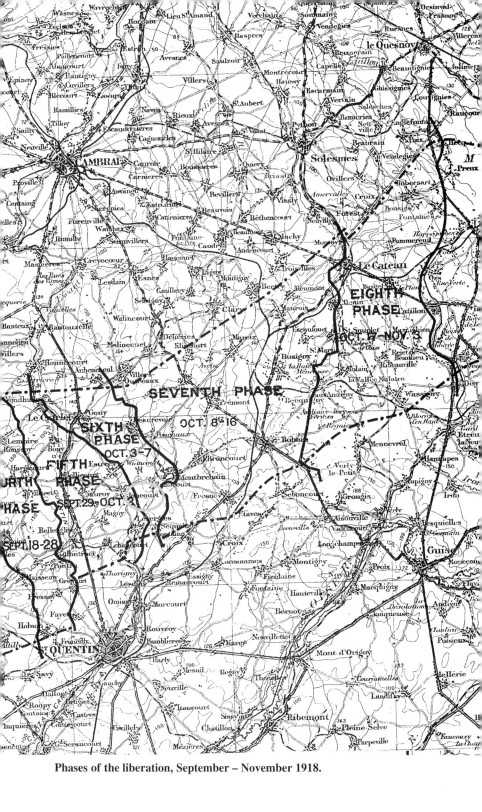

Phases of the liberation, September – November 1918.

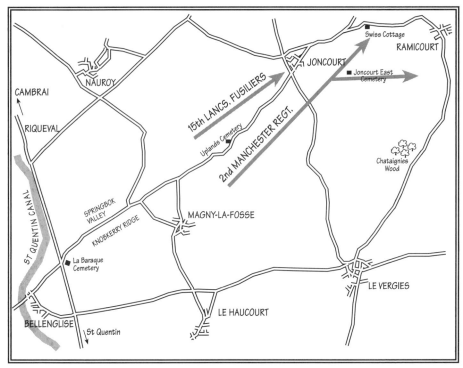

The attack on Joncourt 30 September – 1 October 1918. By the 15 Lancashire Fusiliers and 2nd Manchester Regt.

troubles in your old kit-bag/And smile, smile, smile'). The poem, however, refers to the mental gap between the men with direct experience of the war and those who remained at home.

The feat of breaking the Hindenburg Line on 29 September 1918 by the 46th (North Midland) Division is well known and remains rightly honoured. (The press of the day described it as 'the miracle of the war'.) So too is the exploit of Captain A. H. Charlton, DSO, of 1/6th North Staffs who, with nine of his men, succeeded in capturing the Riqueval Bridge across the St. Quentin canal. It was this division's advance and success in exploiting their victory - penetrating nearly a mile beyond the canal - that enabled the 2nd Manchesters and the 15th and 16th Lancashire Fusiliers to pass through and eventually take up a position further on, just to the east of Magny la Fosse.

On their way there from La Neuville, the Manchesters moved first to Vendelles, a village west of Bellenglise. They were therefore in place ready for a further advance and an attack on the Beaurevoir-Fonsomme line at Joncourt, although by the time they reached Magny La Fosse, east of the canal, on 30 September they had suffered 24 casualties, including four of Owen's brother officers.

At 8 am on 30 September the 15th Lancashire Fusiliers (1st Salford Pals) undertook the initial attack on Joncourt. Attacking from the south-west side of the village, they had the support of an artillery barrage and the help of some tanks; this was undoubtedly necessary, for the outskirts of Joncourt were protected by a number of concrete bunkers, the remains of which can still be seen today. In addition, the defenders were able to shelter behind a railway embankment which curved through the edge of the village. Help from Australian forces which were expected to attack on the left of the battalion did not materialise, and despite repeated and determined attacks the Lancashire Fusiliers were unable to enter the village.

Their attack had not been in vain, however, for the battalion inflicted heavy casualties on the defending enemy forces. Moreover, not only had it established itself on the outskirts of the village but it had made contact with the units on its flanks. Indeed, the Germans were so shaken that when the battalion resumed its attack at 8.30 am on 1 October it was able to clear the village and establish a line beyond it to the east.

Visit: Starting from St. Quentin, take the N44 towards Cambrai for about 6 miles. Very shortly after crossing the St. Quentin canal there is a cross-roads, the road from the left coming from Bellenglise. Take the right turn here, along a narrow road which is easily identified by the CWGC sign indicating the way to La Baraque British cemetery. Carry on past this small cemetery; on the left-hand side of the road, in the valley below, is the location from where Owen and the 2nd Manchesters went forward at 8.30 am on 29 September 1918, on their way to Magny La Fosse.

The turning to Magny La Fosse, to the right, comes soon after, but

Defensive bunker facing west from the railway embankment, Joncourt.

keep straight on. It should be possible to see the Cross of Sacrifice at Uplands Cemetery about half a mile ahead, where Owen's friend Gregg is buried. The view from the cemetery gate, to both left and right, gives an idea of the distance to be covered by the attacking British to reach their objective of Joncourt, and their vulnerability to enemy fire as they did so. Continue for a few hundred yards.

Just before the road enters Joncourt village, pause and look half-left: among the trees that mark the curving line of an old railway embankment, running along the west side of the village above the long slope, it should be possible to make out a German bunker built into the embankment. This is one of the series of bunkers which held the village against the 15th Lancashire Fusiliers on 30 September 1918. Continue slowly towards the village: it is easy to see where the railway line used to cross the road.

Walk: The former permanent way has now been turned into a woodland walk. Leave the car and turn left along the path; the German fortification is soon visible, built into the embankment on the left-hand side and almost hidden by bushes. It is well worth a brief examination. The ground drops away steadily beneath it, and by standing on the bunker roof it is not difficult to imagine the devastating effect of fire from here on the Lancashire Fusiliers.

Return to the car and drive into the village, carry on straight across the D.71 road and park the car beside the village church.

A section of the Beaurevoir-Fonsomme Line (or, as Owen's friend Second Lieutenant Foulkes called it, 'a second Hindenburg Line') stretched along high ground to the east of Joncourt, approximately half a mile from the village itself, running north-west/south-east and almost parallel with the eastern edge of the village. Between the village and the crest of this high ground the land slopes down and then gradually upwards to the top of the ridge where the German defences were established. Although not of the same strength as the main Hindenburg Line, for some trenches had not been fully dug, they were nevertheless by no means insignificant, and in effect represented the final support system of the Hindenburg Line itself. It included numerous well-sited

Joncourt from the Beaurevoir-Fonsomme line, showing how the defence positions along the ridge dominated the village.

The attack Joncourt, 29 September - 2 October 1918.

8 AUS.
Relieved by 5 AUS.
Night Oct 1

COUNTER ATTACK

Wiancourt

Swiss Cottage

Corps Boundary Oct 1 and 2

Joncourt

6 p.m. Sept 29

96

96

The ridge east of Joncourt, with surviving concrete gun-emplacments visible on the horizon.

GUN EMPLACEMENTS

Swiss Cottage, 1918, showing the trench line stretching northwards from the farm.

concrete machine gun posts and rifle pits, some of which are occasionally visible today when the ground is clear of crops.

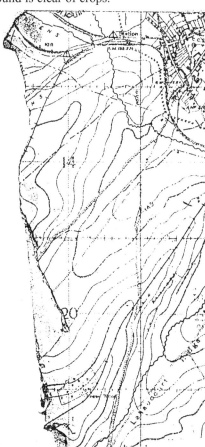

To the north-east of the village, and forming part of these defences, was Moulin Grisons Farm, known to the British as 'Swiss Cottage'. It was the capture of this position and the other German defences along the ridge that was assigned to the 2nd Manchesters on 1 October 1918.

Attacking at 4 pm on a two-company front (one of which was Owen's D Company) under Captain Somerville and helped by several tanks, the Manchesters met with great success and the breakthrough of the enemy's defences was achieved. The defending German soldiers in these emplacements could dominate the valley between the ridge and the village of Joncourt, and the Manchesters had a challenging fight to seize the high ground from them. Owen and his

Swiss Cottage, the same field photographed in 1997. The old trench line across the field is just visible.

John Foulkes's map, showing defences round Joncourt and the defensive German position along the Beaurevoir-Fonsomme line.

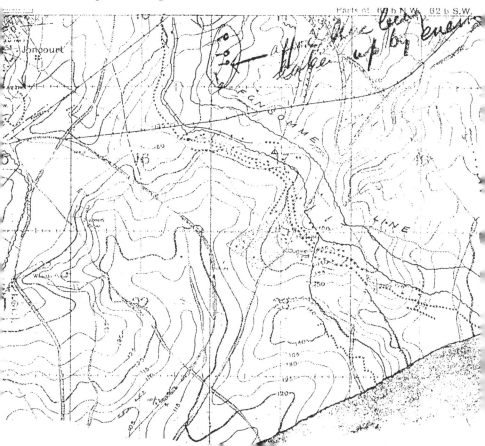

troops attacked up the hill, which was not so open as today, for it was still divided up into small fields by hedges which provided a measure of protection. When one of the tanks was hit and the whole crew except the commander were casualties, another officer and a soldier from the battalion took their places and the tank continued, with considerable success. With stiff hand-to-hand fighting the Manchesters forced their way through thick barbed wire and finally cleared the German line for about 1400 yards stretching south from Swiss Cottage. The group led by Owen seized one of the machine-guns and its crew - and were then pinned down and unable to move on, or back, because of enemy fire.

Walk through to the far end of the village cemetery behind the church, and look straight ahead. Depending on the state of the ground and crops, it may be possible to see the remains of the German bunkers on the ridge, forming the section of the Beaurevoir-Fonsomme line attacked by the 2nd Manchesters on 1 October 1918. This British attack came from the right hand side of the valley in front of you. It was the successful attack on these machine-gun emplacements that won Wilfred Owen his Military Cross.

Look half-left along the ridge. The large farm surrounded by poplar trees is Moulin Grisons Farm, referred to on British army maps and in records as 'Swiss Cottage'. The German counter-attacks came from this area, and it was here that Lieutenant L. H. Smith, MGC, won his Military Cross.

The village cemetery contains some British war graves. At the far right hand corner as you approach from the car is the grave of 266406 Private A. E. Bacon, Notts & Derby Regiment, killed in action on 3 October 1918. His grave stands alone now, but originally it was surrounded by villagers' graves; over the years these plots were not maintained and are now abandoned. According to local memories, Private Bacon's body was found by Chinese labourers clearing the battlefield and buried here.

As you come into the cemetery, other British graves lie on the left. Here can be seen a private memorial to Captain Archibald W. Field of the Royal Flying Corps, who was killed on 9 January 1918 while flying over enemy lines.

CWGC Headstones: Second Lieutenant W. S. Smith. The aircraft in which these two officers (Field and Smith) were flying was a Bristol F2B of No. 48 Squadron. It was attacked in the air by enemy aircraft near Estrées in the morning of 9 January 1918. The aircraft wings were shot away, the aircraft plunged out of control, and both pilot and observer were killed.

Private Bacon, an isolated CWGC grave in Joncourt communal cemetery.

Captain C. L. Graves, of the Nova Scotia Regiment, attached to No. 9 Squadron. The Royal Flying Corps suffered heavy casualties during reconnaissance and bombing operations before and during the Battle of Arras in April 1917 - indeed, it became known to the Flying Corps as 'bloody April'. This officer was one of these victims. Not only was he a casualty of this dangerous work, he was the pilot of one of five aircraft shot down on the same day by Leutnant F. O. Bernert of Jagdstaffel 2.

Just after dawn on 24 April 1917, BE 2e aircraft of No. 9 Squadron RFC took off on a bombing raid. Over Le Catelet they were attacked by German single seater fighters. In the ensuing 'dog-fight' three of the squadron planes were shot down by Leutnant Bernert. The body of the pilot of one of the aircraft, Second Lieutenant F. A. Matthews, was never found, and his name is recorded on the Arras memorial. The second aircraft shot down by Bernert was piloted by Lieutenant G. E. Hicks. He was more fortunate, survived the crash and was taken prisoner. Captain Graves's plane was set on fire and he was burned to death. Bernert's score of British planes shot down that day reached five when he shot down a DH4 from No. 55 Squadron and a Sopwith Strutter from No. 70 Squadron.

It was now late in the day of 1 October, and during the night the German defenders made repeated counter attacks against the battalion's flanks: the Manchesters faced such pressure that a company from the 15th Lancashire Fusiliers came to their support. The Manchesters held the ground that they had gained. This was one of the most advanced and successful onslaughts on the German lines at this time, so that the British troops holding the gun-positions on the ridge were among the farthest forward of any along the Western Front.

They were also helped considerably by a unit of the Machine Gun Corps, under the command of Lieutenant L. H. Smith. Two of his machine guns had been put out of action by an intensive barrage just ahead of one of the enemy counter-attacks; extricating those of his teams who were uninjured, he pushed forward four of his guns to some advanced posts near Swiss Cottage and by engaging the enemy at close range succeeded in fending off the threat to the Manchesters' left flank. He was awarded the Military Cross for his gallantry and what the citation describes as 'good work'. Captain Somerville, Owen's very likeable Company Commander, was wounded during the struggle for the ridge outside Joncourt, and Owen, as the senior surviving officer in the company, took command for the rest of the company's action and then led the men away from the battlefield - for which he later received tremendous praise and admiration from his friend and brother officer Second Lieutant Foulkes.

John Foulkes was in Owen's Company for the attack at Joncourt, and also at Ors on 4 November 1918, where he was wounded. Having joined up in January 1915 in the South Lancashire Regiment, he was commissioned in 1918 and travelled from Etaples with Owen in September 1918. Like Owen, he won the Military Cross for his actions at Joncourt. Later he became Headmaster of a Stockport school. Edmund Blunden interviewed him some years afterwards for the lengthy memoir he wrote to accompany his influential 1931 edition of Owen's poetry.

These successes and in the general British advance elsewhere were, however, not without sacrifice, and some of Owen's friends were amongst the Joncourt battle casualties.

Lieutenant Gregg, who had been with Owen in Scarborough, died of his wounds, and Second Lieutenant Potts was wounded.

Gregg, who was 38, is buried in Uplands Cemetery, on the approach to Joncourt from Magny la Fosse. He and Owen had known each other at Scarborough. Another officer wounded at this time was Captain Samuel Watts, an original member of the 20th Battalion Manchester Regiment and attached to the Trench Mortar battery. Evacuated to England, he was later to die of his wounds at Millbank Hospital in London. Afterwards his body was interred in the family vault in a churchyard at Heaton Mersey (Stockport) Congregational church. In due time the burial ground was covered by a car park! When this was brought to the attention of the CWGC, a suitably worded headstone commemorating Captain Watts was placed near the car park.

Uplands cemetery, south-west of Joncourt. Lieutenant Gregg is buried here. The picture shows the exposed open valley approaching Joncourt.

Owen himself survived unscathed, and was almost exhilarated to find his nerves steady - it was his first experience of front-line action since the Manchesters were outside St. Quentin seventeen months earlier and the subsequent shell-shock. In view of his close relationship with his mother, it is not surprising that he was quick to write to her about the stirring events outside Joncourt:

> *As you must have known both by my silence and from the newspapers which mention this Division ... I have been in action*

Joncourt school and mairie, used by the German forces as their local headquarters throughout the 1914-18 occupation.

The effects of two days of battle: Joncourt church in 1920, before reconstruction.

for some days. I can find no word to qualify my experiences except the word SHEER. (Curiously enough I find the papers talk about sheer fighting!) It passed the limits of my Abhorrence. I lost all my earthly faculties, and fought like an angel. If I started into detail of our engagement I should disturb the censor and my own Rest. You will guess what has happened when I say I am now Commanding the Company, and in the line had a boy lance-corporal as my Sergeant-Major. With this corporal who stuck to me and shadowed me like your prayers I captured a German Machine Gun and scores of prisoners. I'll tell you exactly how another time. I only shot one man with my revolver (at about 30 yards!); the rest I took with a smile. The same thing happened with other parties all along the line we entered. [4th or 5th October 1918]

A few days later, his next letter expanded a little:

You will understand I could not write - when you think of us for days all but surrounded by the enemy. All one day (afer the battle) we could not move from a small trench, though hour by hour the wounded were groaning just outside. Three stretcher-bearers who got up were hit, one after one. I had to order no one to show himself after that ... I scrambled out myself and felt an exhilaration in baffling the Machine Guns by quick bounds from cover to cover. After the shells we had been through, and the gas,

Congratulations from the Commanding Officer of the 2nd Manchesters after the Joncourt attack.

> bullets were like the gentle rain from heaven ... Must now write
> to hosts of parents of Missing, etc. [8 October 1918]

He also wrote to Sassoon, referring to his feelings during the battle and the period spent pinned down before they could return to the battalion, and commenting:

> I'm glad I've been recommended for M.C., and hope I get it,
> for the confidence it may give me at home. Full of confidence
> after having taken a few machine guns (with the help of one
> seraphic lance corporal), I held a most glorious brief peace talk
> in a pill box. [10 October 1918]

As Owen indicated in his letters, the Manchesters' success in capturing this section of the German defences was not to go unrewarded. Within his first two weeks of active service, Owen remarked to his mother of the Victoria Cross that 'I covet it not' (letter, 10 January 1917), but when he learned of the recommendation for his Military Cross he felt vindicated in his nerves and steadiness, and happy that his leadership had been so successful:

> I have been recommended for the Military Cross; and have
> recommended every single N.C.O. who was with me! My nerves
> are in perfect order. I came out in order to help these boys -

directly by leading them as well as an officer can; indirectly, by watching their sufferings that I may speak of them as well as a pleader can. I have done the first. [4th/5th October 1918]

Describing it as a 'crowning success', recommendations by the battalion for Military Crosses, and Bars where appropriate, were submitted for consideration with the names of the two Second Lieutenants, Owen and Foulkes, included. In Owen's case, the citation read as follows: For conspicuous gallantry and devotion to duty in the

attack on the Fonsomme Line on 1st/2nd October 1918. On the Company Commander becoming a casualty, he assumed command and showed fine leadership and resisted a heavy counter-attack. He personally manipulated a captured enemy Machine Gun from an

Soldiers moving forward in pursuit of the German army on 9 October 1918. This photograph was taken near Joncourt, which had been captured 1 October, and shows the open country and the undamaged roads on which the pursuit was by that time being carried on.

isolated position and inflicted considerable losses on the enemy. Throughout he behaved most gallantly.

> **Visit:** Return to the car, drive down past the church and turn right along the D.713. About half a mile down the road, the parking space and path to Joncourt East CWGC cemetery lie on the right, its graves holding some of the men of the Manchesters and the Lancashire Fusiliers who fell here during the October battle. Continue up the hill for another quarter-mile, to Moulin Grisons Farm (Swiss Cottage) on the right of the road. It was from the left hand side of the road here that the Germans mounted repeated counter attacks against the Manchesters during the night of 1 October 1918.
>
> Going forward, the road enters Ramicourt, the village attacked by the 16th Lancashire Fusiliers on 2 October 1918. Their commanding officer, Lieutenant-Colonel Arthur Stone, was killed in this attack. Follow the signs to Montbrehain and then along the D.282 to the main D.932 road and turn right. This leads to Le Cateau some 15 miles further on.

Meanwhile, others in the Brigade were called forward to harry the retreating enemy, and the Manchesters withdrew westwards.

Notes & Sources

Breaking the Hindenberg Line. The Story of the 46th (North Midland) Division, R. E. Priestly, T. Fisher Unwin Ltd., 1919

The Sky Their Battlefied, T. Henshaw, Grub Street, 1995

The Hindenburg Line, Peter Oldham, 'Battleground Europe' series (Leo Cooper, 1997)

Chapter Five

THE CANAL ATTACK AT ORS

On 2 October, the day when Wilfred Owen brought his men safely out of the captured machine-gun post, the 16th Battalion Lancashire Fusiliers entered the battle. After forming up to the east of Joncourt they advanced towards their objective, the village of Ramicourt which lay just beyond the newly-captured Beaurevoir-Fonsomme line. The attack was not successful, for their left flank had not been secured and the battalion suffered heavy casualties. Amongst those killed was the Commanding Officer, Lieutenant-Colonel A. Stone, DSO, who had joined the 15th battalion in 1914.

On 3 October the 2nd Manchesters' relief arrived, and the battalion made its way back to the west, and into dugouts on the banks of the St.Quentin canal. This proved to be a costly retirement, for during the withdrawal they suffered some 23 men killed, another 70 wounded, and 20 missing.

Three days later they were back in Hancourt. Here they set about a general clean-up of kit and equipment and – very necessary after the recent battle – a reorganisation of companies, platoons and sections. Owen was pleased to see a draft arrive from Scarborough, most of it assigned to Owen's company, of which he was temporarily in command. Some of the reinforcements were men whom he remembered from Scarborough – waiters when he was running the Mess in 1917 at the Clarence Gardens Hotel – and he chose one of them, Private Roberts, to replace his servant. The officer draft included Second Lieutenant James Kirk of the 10th Manchesters, recently attached for duty with the 2nd battalion. He was to win the Victoria Cross almost exactly a month later on the Sambre-Oise canal, and to lose his life there.

As befits a unit with regimental pride, the 16th Lancashire Fusiliers had brought away the body of their Commanding Officer from Ramicourt where he was killed, for burial in Hancourt cemetery. The Manchesters' Corps of Drums attended, as did Owen and his fellow officers of the 2nd Manchesters. Lieutenant-Colonel Stone's replacement was announced as Major J. N. Marshall (he of the ten wounds, as Owen described him), who took over as commanding officer with the rank of Lieutenant-Colonel. The position of second in command of the Manchesters was filled by Major J. L. Murphy, who

Hancourt British cemetery. Wilfred Owen attended the funeral here of Lt-Col. Stone, after his death at Ramicourt.

had travelled with Owen in the officer draft from Etaples in September.

While here, Owen wrote to Sassoon about the action at Joncourt, and also mentioned an acquaintance, Conal O'Riordan, whom he had met a month earlier at Etaples. In 1909 O'Riordan, an Irish man of letters, became director of the famous Abbey Theatre in Dublin. He ran the Y.M.C.A. hut at Etaples base camp. Of Owen, he wrote later:

I know that he paid me his first visit about tea-time on a sunny day in early September, 1918, and he was gone again up the line before the month was out. But while he was at the base, he must have come to see me almost every day. So it is that I see so clearly his charming face; a child's despite the tiny moustache, smiling at me in the sunlight or under the rays of the swinging lamp he would light for me when I drew the curtains at evenfall. Although he must have been in his twenty-sixth year (the age of Major Bonaparte at Toulon), he seemed quite the youngest officer who came my way...he confessed himself to me deeply bitten by the heresy that the Germans, however grievously to blame, were no more so than ourselves and our allies, if even so much could be claimed...

Although O'Riordan and Owen discussed Sassoon and his poetry, Owen could not be persuaded to show any of his own work, although at the time he was writing 'Smile, Smile, Smile', and completing 'The Sentry' and 'Exposure'. The latter, with its atmospheric mood and repeated statement that

98

After their rest period, the 2nd Manchesters were on the move again on 18 October. By now it was possible to think of the end of the war as a real possibility – what Owen called a 'rumble on the horizon' – and he no doubt remembered his 'most glorious brief peace talk' while pinned down in the captured machine-gun post at Joncourt. But there was still work to be done first, and the 2nd Manchesters resumed their march eastward in pursuit of the enemy via Bohain-en-Vermandois, Busigny and St. Souplet towards Le Cateau.

A contemporary sketch of Le Cateau during the occupation. *(Paul Seret)*

More than four years earlier the 2nd Manchesters took part in the retreat from Mons and were involved in the epic stand at Le Cateau on 26 August 1914. (It figures in the Regiment's battle honours.) As they approached the town on 30 October 1918, crossing over the main Cambrai road on their way to Pommereuil, was there anyone in the battalion who could remember the alarming casualties of that fateful day in 1914, most of whom had to be left in the very fields the battalion was now skirting?

Surprisingly, even at this late stage in the war and amongst the 18- and 19-year-old conscripts now marching to battle, there were at least two Other Rank veterans who had been at Le Cateau in 1914. Both men – Acting Corporal Syrett, MM, and Private Massey – were to be killed on the banks of the Sambre-Oise canal in five days' time. Today they lie in good company, their graves in Ors communal cemetery being in the same row as those of Wilfred Owen, Second Lieutenant Kirk, VC, and Lieutenant-Colonel Marshall, VC. These veterans share the ground with some of the young recent conscripts.

Visit: Before leaving for Ors it is worth finding your way to a memorial outside the town, erected to commemorate those who fought here on 26 August 1914 and including the 2nd Manchesters. The memorial is not easy to find, but the following instructions may be helpful:

From the cross-roads junction of the N43 and D.932 roads, about half

Christmas card of Le Cateau, 1918.

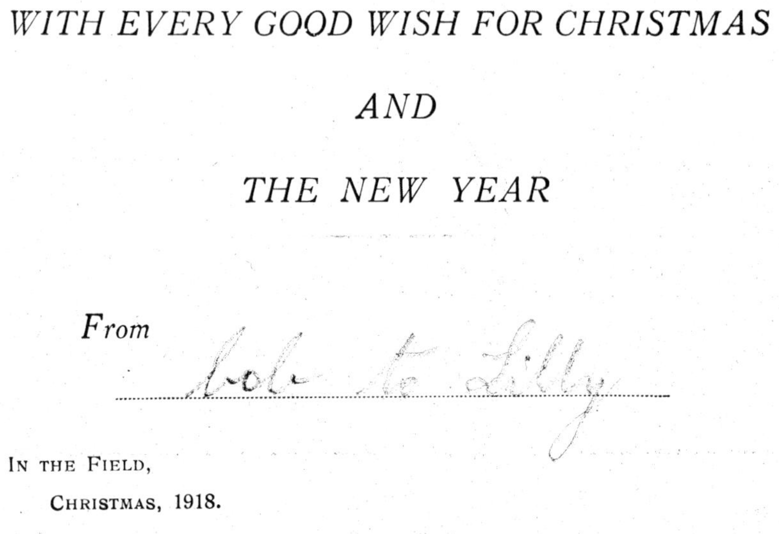

WITH EVERY GOOD WISH FOR CHRISTMAS

AND

THE NEW YEAR

From

Iol to Lilly

In the Field,

Christmas, 1918.

General Sir Horace Smith-Dorrien unveiling Le Cateau Memorial in May 1926.

a mile to the west of Le Cateau, drive down the hill towards the town. At the first cross-roads turn right and continue to the T-junction. Turn left and at the next (almost immediate) cross-roads, turn right. Very shortly, turn right to the 'Complexe Sportif'. Leave the car here and continue on foot up the track ahead: the memorial is soon visible on top of the hill, in the middle of a clump of trees ahead.

To continue to Ors, leave Le Cateau on the main N.43 road, heading east. Pass under the railway bridge and, as the road leaves the town, turn left on to the small D.959, to the village of Pommereuil. The road crosses a small stream, the Richemont, which in summer is barely noticeable – but on 23 October 1918, as the advancing troops made for Pommereuil, it was four feet deep. Just to get across this small brook meant that the engineers had to construct no fewer than fourteen bridges.

It was 31 October when Owen and his men reached Pommereuil, about two miles north–east of Le Cateau. The Field Ambulance established here was used as a collecting post for wounded who were sent on to Le Cateau and beyond; others brought in were many French civilians in a very feeble condition from age, sickness, gas poisoning, and the shortage of food during the long German occupation.

Here too was one of the battalions relieved by the Manchesters, the 4th Battalion King's Shropshire Light Infantry – the Territorial Force battalion based on Owen's home town of Shrewsbury. Pommereuil had been captured a week earlier by two other battalions of the Manchester Regiment, the 20th and 21st battalions which were the original 5th and 6th Manchester 'Pals'. Their attack here, to the west of the Sambre-Oise canal on the edge of a large stretch of woodland, had cost the former Pals battalions a number of casualties as they 'winkled' the enemy out of it. Many of the trees had been cut down by the Germans during the occupation, with much of the felling and clearing work undertaken by forced labour gangs of Russian prisoners of war, who were accommodated in camps in the nearby village of Ors.[1] Just over a mile away to the east was the canal, and in the fields beside it, about 1000 yards north of Ors, the 2nd Manchesters were to assemble before attacking across the canal into the German defences on the far bank.

Visit: Go straight through Pommereuil and continue towards Landrecies. Just beyond the village the road enters the forest where the 2nd Manchesters rested before their attack on the canal at Ors on 4 November 1918. (The high wire fences surround a modern military camp.) At the far end of the wire and close to the camp entrance on the right, note a house with the name Maison Forestière (Forestry House) over the door; it was in the cellar of this house that Owen wrote his final letter home. Continue along the D.959 road towards Landrecies, and take the right turn about a quarter of a mile beyond the camp entrance. This small road, C.5, leads into the woodland and is also marked by the usual CWGC cemetery sign.

 During the Second World War, General Rommel met strong resistance near Pommereuil from French troops. On 18 May 1940 he failed to get past a few French heavy tanks barring his way to Le Cateau; he therefore reversed direction and diverted via the narrow C.5 road towards Ors, overwhelmed the opposition that he encountered there, and continued through the village before pressing on to Le Cateau and thence to Cambrai and Arras.

1. In Mormal Forest not far away, an elephant was used for part of the war to help with the timber felling and extraction.

It was clear that the end of the war was approaching, and the forthcoming attack was to be the last substantial engagement undertaken by the 2nd Manchesters. Lieutenant-Colonel Marshall, who was highly regarded by the 32nd Division, was asked to undertake a reconnaissance on its behalf. He expressed considerable criticism of its final orders; his own battalion, the 16th Lancashire Fusiliers, had been given the almost impossible task of crossing the Sambre-Oise canal and charging up a rising slope to attack and capture their objective, the stoutly defended La Motte Farm. The artillery barrage and continuing fire, Marshall was told, would eliminate all opposition. He feared a repetition of the opening of the Battle of the Somme, when confident claims that troops could advance without opposition – the enemy's positions having been eliminated by artillery fire – proved tragically false; unfortunately his concern proved to be well-founded.

Clearly, crossing the canal would not be easy. All bridges had been destroyed by the enemy, from bank to bank it was about 21 metres wide (about 12 metres at water level), and it was bordered by ditches about 4 metres wide and filled with water. The canal itself was some 2 metres deep, the bottom being soft mud. In Ors itself the canal went through a 5-metre wide lock with a bridge, now partly demolished. The landscape around Ors is very different from the broad uplands of the Somme; it remains a region of copses and small low-lying fields, used for cattle rather than arable crops. The Germans had flooded some of the fields round Ors, turning them into a swamp. The ground to the west – British – side of the canal consisted of small orchards in thick hedges. Observation and maintaining direction in the forthcoming attack would not be straightforward.

The 2nd Manchesters rested while the plans were being drawn up, and Owen was fortunate to find shelter in the crowded cellar of the forestry house. During the early evening of 31 October 1918, surrounded by sleeping officers, officers' servants, cooks and a signaller, he found time to write to his mother from what he describes as his 'smoky cellar'. This was to be the last of his many letters: like the vast majority of its predecessors, it was addressed to Susan Owen, and it therefore seems appropriate that she should be the recipient of this final communication.

Visit: The woodland to the left of the C.5 road towards Ors is where the 2nd Manchesters' A and B Companies waited in reserve during the battle of 4 November. It was from here that, following C and D Companies' unsuccessful attack, they set off into Ors to cross the canal lower down, using the 1st Dorsets' bridge.

The forester's house between Pommereuil and Ors.

Carry on along the road and over the railway level crossing.

Walk: Just beyond the level crossing, the CWGC sign indicates the location of Ors British cemetery, a few hundred yards away to the left. Walk through the two fields to the cemetery, where the register also includes the details of men buried in the Ors communal cemetery (including Wilfred Owen). It was from this area that in the early hours of 4 November 1918 Owen's D Company made their final advance towards the canal bank, with C Company on their right. The canal is visible, lined with trees beyond another small field.

The view from Ors British cemetery towards the canal, hidden by the trees, and the 2nd Manchesters D Company position.

Return to the car and continue along the road for about 300 yards. C and D Companies lined up at their start line on the left here, in some cases parallel with the road, ready for the attack.

Stop at the road junction. Both of the roads ahead lead into Ors village.

Walk: Before taking the left-hand fork, park the car and walk down the little lane to the left immediately before the fork, which leads down to the canal bank, named at the corner with a sign, 'Rue Verte Vallée'. In the early morning of 4 November it formed part of the route taken by the right flank of the 2nd Manchesters. Walking over the footbridge at the end, over the stream running alongside the canal, you will be crossing some of the ditches which had to be bridged by the Engineers so that the Manchesters could reach the canal and line its bank.

As you stand on the canal bank looking across the water you are occupying the position where C Company of the Manchesters took up their position in the early hours of 4 November. La Motte Farm can be seen at the top of the rising field on the far side of the canal, overlooking the land that the Manchesters were expected to seize. About 300 yards to your left is the spot where D Company and Wilfred Owen went into action and where Owen was killed. About the same distance to your right is the lock and bridge over it, the gap which in 1918 the Engineers hoped to cover by floating a pontoon carrying a span of bridge down the canal and into the lock.

The attack and crossing of the canal would depend on the effectiveness and superiority of the British artillery and other fire-power over the Germans facing them on the eastern bank of the canal. The British barrage was arranged in a series of 'lifts' with various timed pauses so as to bring fire to bear on the German side of the canal. There would, however, be a 300-metre gap on the enemy's side of the canal, to be left untouched by shell-fire; this was to avoid breaching the edge of the canal bank and thereby flooding the low ground behind it and offering a further obstacle to the attackers. The drawback was that the German machine-guns must therefore be eliminated by other means, no simple task.

A vital element in the success of the whole operation was to be provided by the 206th and 218th Field Companies of the Royal Engineers. Their task was to construct rafts and bridges so that the attacking units could first negotiate the wide ditch beside the canal and then get across the canal itself to form a bridgehead on the far bank. In addition they were required to bridge the gap at Ors lock for the 1st Battalion Dorsetshire Regiment (14th Brigade); this involved constructing a pontoon upon which a span of bridge could be floated down the canal and into the lock.

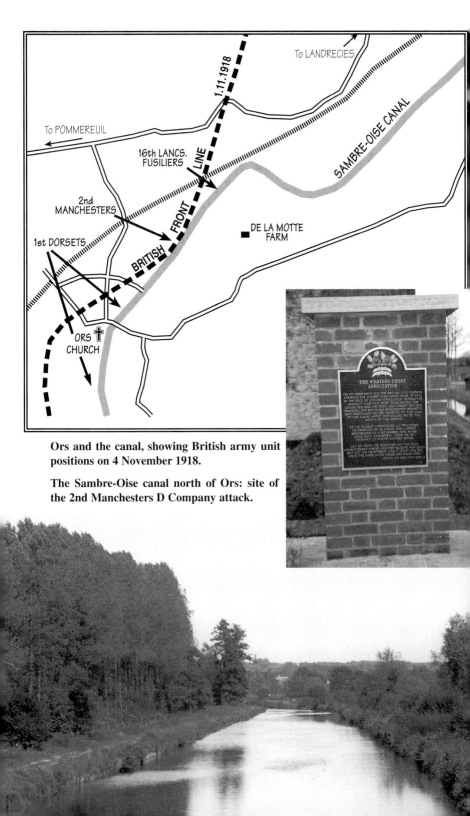

To LANDRECIES

1.11.1918

To POMMEREUIL

SAMBRE-OISE CANAL

16th LANCS. FUSILIERS

FRONT LINE

2nd MANCHESTERS

DE LA MOTTE FARM

1st DORSETS

BRITISH LINE

ORS CHURCH

Ors and the canal, showing British army unit positions on 4 November 1918.

The Sambre-Oise canal north of Ors: site of the 2nd Manchesters D Company attack.

In their attack on the canal and on up the slope beyond, the Manchesters and the Lancashire Fusiliers were to be supported by 218 Field Company, RE, commanded by Major Arnold Waters. Two floating bridges made up of empty kerosene tins were planned, constructed by the 42 men of Major Waters's three sections who were assisted in their turn by A Company of the 16th Battalion Highland Light Infantry (City of Glasgow Regt.). This battalion had faced disbandment in February 1918 as part of the reduction in the unit strength in each brigade, but with the consent of its commanding officer the 16th HLI had become the 32nd Division's much-needed Pioneers. Like the Royal Engineers, the HLI were to suffer severe casualties in the forthcoming battle.

Visit: Return to your car, take the left fork into the village, and park in the open space in front of the church and the Mairie. Take the small footpath to the right of the church and pause for a moment to read the inscriptions on the plaque on the wall. They tell a vivid story of the impact of the Second World War on the village, its inhabitants and its temporary

The creeping barrage plan for the attack on 4 November 1918.

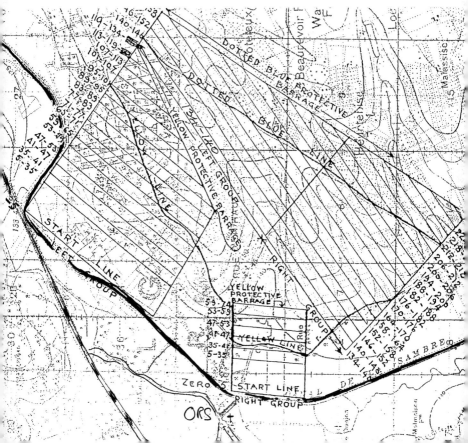

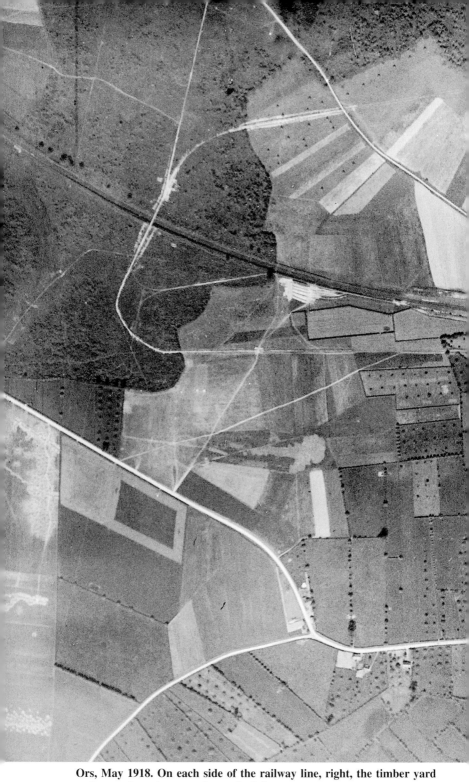

Ors, May 1918. On each side of the railway line, right, the timber yard and camp for prisoners who worked there.

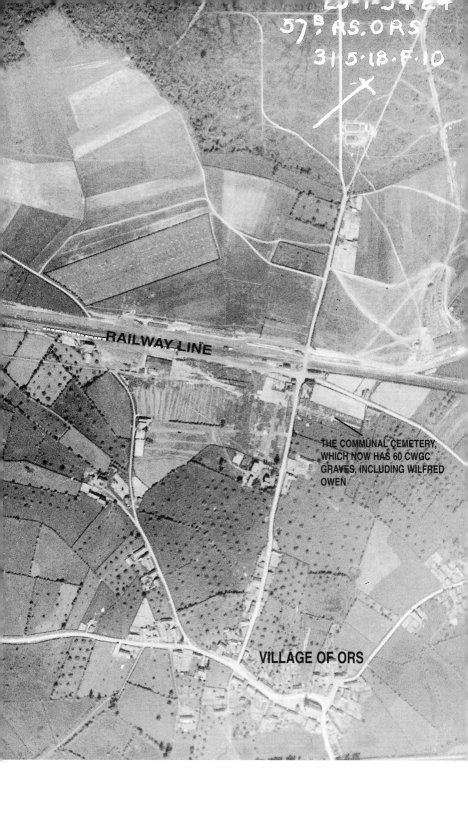

RAILWAY LINE

THE COMMUNAL CEMETERY,
WHICH NOW HAS 60 CWGC
GRAVES, INCLUDING WILFRED
OWEN

VILLAGE OF ORS

refugee residents. It includes a list of those killed in the defence of Ors on 18 May 1940, when the village was attacked by Rommel and his Panzer column.

Walk on to the bridge, and note the plaque presented by the Western Front Assocation to the village in memory of all those who fought here on 4 November 1918, mentioning Wilfred Owen by name and including a stanza from his poem 'With an Identity Disc'. Standing by the bridge with the memorial at your right hand, you will see the canal bending to left as it continues southwards. The floating bridge used by Lt. Robins and the 1st Dorsets to cross the canal was located a short way beyond the bend, the move which led to the final success of the attack on the 4 November 1918.

Return to your car.

The Civilian Population of Ors. Until now, the village residents had escaped the most obvious dangers of warfare, for the Western Front during the static years of the war ran far to the west of them. By now, however, they were suffering from the effects of deprivation (food and livestock shortages, which made family and farming life increasingly difficult, many of the male workforce absent on forced labour), and the Spanish Flu pandemic had hit the community hard. The second wave of infection hit the area in September and October 1918, reaching its peak around early November and continuing until April 1919. Refugees from Montbrehain, driven out by the advancing front, reached Ors in October with many elderly and sick people who were lodged in the church. There were too many deaths for the undertakers and joiners to keep up with coffin-making; some families brought in planks of their own to make their dead relative's coffin, and the German authorities arranged some mass burials with the addition of quick-lime to prevent further infection. Nearly 40 flu deaths were recorded in Ors during October 1918 – and in the midst of this wave of illness, the village was shelled with increasing intensity: on 13 October the Germans ordered a general evacuation. On foot, in carts, sick or well, most departed, although a few were too ill to travel or insisted on staying in their cellars. A number of people died on their way to safety. By 4 November the village was virtually empty.

The British troops at Bazuel (on the main road east out of Le Cateau, about 2 miles from Ors) were shelled from mid-October onwards and the two air forces were engaged in battle overhead on 14 October. Closer to the canal, the Germans dug a trench through the village providing cover for approaching the canal bank, and added a temporary footbridge over the canal to link the remaining outposts with the remainder of their forces on the east bank. The German army was not quite beaten yet, their machine-gun crews were as brave and resolute as ever, and in the attack of 4 November the Manchesters were faced by Prussian soldiers, renowned for their tenacity in battle.

In the first two days of November the land to the north of Ors, along the canal bank towards Landrecies, had to be cleared in a series of attacks and counter-attacks. The last of the outposts was cleared on Saturday 2 November, and as the final groups of German troops withdrew they dismantled the footbridge behind them. The 2nd Manchesters shifted to their position near the banks of the canal, about 1000 yards north of the Ors lock, with the 16th Lancashire Fusiliers under Lieutenant-Colonel Marshall on their left.

In the early hours of 4 November the Dorsets extended their coverage of the canal bank to close the gap between them and the Manchesters to their left. From north to south, the British units were now therefore in the sequence of 16th Lancashires, 2nd Manchesters and 1st Dorsets. The latter's plan of action was to cross the canal by spanning the gap in the damaged bridge at the lock, and also by a floating bridge which the sappers of 206 Field Coy. RE were to throw across the water at a point some 200 yards south of the lock. As part of the support for this operation, the Dorsets had a field gun placed where it could fire point blank at the damaged bridge. All was now ready.

The British artillery began its barrage at 5.45 am on 4 November 1918, a misty morning. When this covering mist cleared the day was reasonably good for flying, and the opposing air forces confronted each other in perhaps the last great air contest of the war. The strength and activity of the RAF prevented the German air forces from undertaking serious attacks on the British ground troops along the canal. On the ground however, heavy enemy fire frustrated the RE's brave attempt to float a span of bridge down the canal to the lock and the Dorsets were therefore unable to cross the canal at this narrow point as planned. During their attempt an officer of

the Dorsets, Second Lieutenant Cassalman, was unsuccessful in his effort to cross the canal just north of the lock when his collapsible boat capsized.

Seeing that the spanning of the gap in the lock was not going to work, sappers of 206 Field Coy. RE, accompanied by a platoon of the Dorsets, rushed forward with material to fill the gap in the bridge over the lock; but they were mown down by an enemy machine-gun and a field gun firing straight across the bridge. Meanwhile, five minutes

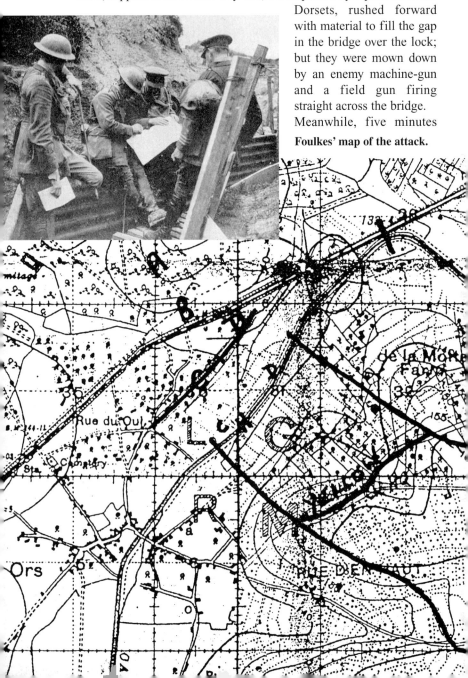

Foulkes' map of the attack.

after the barrage began the 2nd Manchesters dashed forward from their forming-up places in orchards close to the canal. Using planks laid by the engineers across the ditches along the side of the canal, they reached the canal bank itself. Wilfred Owen and his D Company had the 16th Lancashire Fusiliers on their immediate left and the Manchesters' C Company on their right. A and B Companies were held in reserve as support troops, behind them in the forest.

The engineers in the Manchesters' section (218th Field Coy. RE) attempted to launch their floating bridge across the canal, despite intense enemy fire and heavy casualties. In order to give them cover a young officer in the Manchesters, Second Lieutenant Kirk, paddled himself out across the canal on a raft and opened fire with a Lewis gun on the defending German forces. Fresh drums of ammunition were brought out to him – but eventually he was shot in the head and killed.

For his conspicuous courage in the action Second Lieutenant Kirk was posthumously awarded the Victoria Cross.

The engineers succeeded in getting a bridge across, and two platoons of the Manchesters managed to reach the far bank of

Second Lieutenant James Kirk, VC.

German field gun in action.

the canal – but almost immediately the bridge was destroyed by enemy fire, and although repeated attempts were made to repair it, the shelling was so heavy that the engineers were forced to abandon their efforts.

While this furious activity was continuing, the 16th Lancashire Fusiliers were equally and similarly occupied in their sector to the north of the Manchesters. Another group of sappers from 218 Field Company was constructing a second floating bridge. Despite casualties and great difficulties, the engineers completed its construction in half an hour, and one officer and three men managed to get across it to the far bank before the bridge was broken. Lieutenant-Colonel Marshall, the commanding officer, organised parties to repair the bridge, some of whom were killed or wounded. None the less, volunteers continued to come forward to help in its repair and it was eventually completed once more. Marshall took command of a company waiting to go forward and tried to rush across at the head of his men: he was shot in the head and killed instantly. Orders were given that no further attempts to cross were to be made along this stretch of the canal.

Lieutenant-Colonel Marshall was awarded the VC for his gallantry. He and Kirk were not alone in this award for this day's work, for Sapper Archibald and Major Waters of 218 Field Coy. RE also received the award of the Victoria Cross for their bravery under fire whilst working on bridge construction across the canal.[2]

2. After the war, the Lancashire Fusiliers claimed Marshall's award as a VC won by an officer of their Regiment. The War Office, however, ruled that as the colonel belonged to the Irish Guards and was only *attached* to the Lancashire Fusiliers, the award must be credited to the Irish Guards. Reluctantly, therefore, the Fusiliers had to reduce their harvest of VCs won from 18 to 17.

Major A. H. S. Waters, born in 1886, was an engineer, a profession in which he achieved prominence after the war. His Victoria Cross citation included the comment that on hearing that all his officers had been killed or wounded he 'personally supervised the completion of the bridge working on cork floats while under fire at point blank range ... The success of the operation was due entirely to his valour and example'.

However, the 1st Battalion of the Dorsetshire Regiment (14th Brigade), who were holding positions in the village of Ors and close to the canal to the south of the bridge, were more successful. South of the village, protected by covering fire from the Dorsets, Royal Engineers from 206 Field Company built a floating bridge across the canal. Two companies of the Dorsets immediately rushed across, spread out north and south and formed a sizeable bridgehead. The first man across, Second Lieutenant Francis Robins (formerly a cadet in the Artists Rifles, with his name recorded as Francis Rabino) was awarded the Military Cross for his exploit.

By 8.30 am, A and B companies of the 2nd Manchesters and men of the 16th Lancashire Fusiliers moved into Ors and immediately crossed the canal on this floating bridge. They then turned northwards again and resumed the attack on the original objectives, paying particular attention to the enemy forces who were resisting stoutly round La Motte Farm.

Little is known about how Wilfred Owen was killed during the

La Motte Farm today.

The original wooden cross on Owen's grave.

Manchesters' attack. According to his friend John Foulkes, Owen was last seen trying to cross the canal on a raft under very heavy German fire.

This action was the end of the 2nd Manchesters' active war. When the news of the armistice on 11 November reached them they were still

British graves in Ors village cemetery, with the village beyond.

in the same area, in billets to the south of Landrecies, the town that they had entered on 18 August 1914 on their way to Mons. Between these two dates the battalion had lost 44 officers and 1,121 Other Ranks dead, more than any of the other 26 battalions of the Regiment which served overseas in the Great War.

Wilfred Owen's grave is in Ors communal cemetery, where a group of some sixty white CWGC headstones can be found beyond the more sombre granite or marble tombstones and wrought-iron crosses of the village graves. The register is kept at the British cemetery. Owen is in the back row, second from the left and in the same row as Kirk, VC and Marshall, VC.

The battalion second in command, Major Murphy, who travelled with Owen from Etaples to rejoin the battalion in September 1918, survived the day and received a bar to his DSO.

Visit: With your back to the church and the Mairie on your left, set off westwards on the D.160a, and after about 150 yards turn right along the D.160b. About 400 yards along on the right and just before the railway is the village cemetery. The Cross of Sacrifice marking the British burial plot is easily visible. Facing the cemetery gate is the area where huts housed the forced labour employed by the German occupying forces in 1914-18 (including Russian prisoners of war) for felling and processing timber from the nearby forest.

Owen's grave in Ors village cemetery, with its misleading epitaph.

The epitaph on Owen's tombstone is particularly interesting. It was selected by his mother Susan Owen, and comes from his own poem 'The End':

Shall Life renew these bodies? Of a truth
All death will he annul

At first sight this seems to be a clear statement of Christian belief in the after-life and particularly suitable since it was written by the dead man himself – but, as the complete poem shows, his actual meaning is the exact reverse of this apparent expression of faith. The second line, in full, is 'All death will he annul, all tears assuage?' – a question not a statement; and the poem's concluding lines show a clear and defiant denial of war and of an after-life:

When I do ask white Age, he saith not so:

117

'My head hangs weighed with snow.'
And when I hearken to the Earth, she saith:
'My fiery heart shrinks, aching. It is death.
Mine ancient scars shall not be glorified,
Nor my titanic tears, the seas, be dried.'

Return to the car, reverse direction and return towards the village centre. At the T-junction, turn right along the D.160a, forking right after about a mile to Bazuel on the N.43 and then right for Le Cateau.

Harold Owen, Wilfred's brother, stated in his memoirs that the award of the Military Cross was 'immediate', but this was an inaccurate representation of the sequence of events: the recommendation was indeed immediate, but the news of confirmation came through only after Owen was killed. It was recorded in the Manchesters' war diary for 8 November 1918.

Nor did Owen know, when he was killed, that he had become a full Lieutenant exactly eighteen months after being commissioned – the usual period. This information only reached the Owen family after Wilfred's death. Early in 1919, in response to a letter from the War Office referring to Wilfred as Lieutenant Owen, his father wrote to enquire when he had been promoted to that rank. It turned out that he was granted the substantive rank of Lieutenant as from 4 December 1917, and that the promotion had been promulgated on 5 November 1918, the day after his death.

In the decades since his death Wilfred Owen's reputation has grown until he is regarded as perhaps the greatest poet of his era to find inspiration in his war experience and as a spokesman for those who suffer from the cruelties of war. Amongst his poems that are rooted both in one man's experience and in humanity's continuing response to war, 'Futility' (written in May 1918) reflects the apparently pointless loss of life; and 'Anthem for Doomed Youth' can be read as an elegy for the dead of the war and also as a description of the mourning in the Owen family home in Shrewsbury when the news of Wilfred's death reached them on (bitter irony) 11 November 1918. It may be that his final letter, sent to his ailing mother and written in the crowded cellar before the attack on the canal at Ors, provides a fitting epitaph. The modern visitor to the village cemetery in Ors, where the poet lies surrounded by his companions in war, can think of the final lines that reveal his concern for them and for his mother, and his confidence in his achievements and abilities:

Notes & Sources
History of the Dorsetshire Regiment 1914-1919, Ling, 1932

...It is a great life. I am more oblivious than alas! yourself, dear Mother, of the ghastly glimmering of the guns outside, and the hollow crashing of the shells. There is no danger down here, or if any, it will be well over before you read these lines. I hope you are as warm as I am; as serene in your room as I am here; and that you think of me never in bed as resignedly as I think of you always in bed. Of this I am certain you could not be visited by a band of friends half so fine as surround me here.

Shrewsbury Abbey grounds, June 1993: Rehearsal for the unveiling of the memorial 'Symmetry' (by Paul de Monchaux), by children from the Wilfred Owen school, Shrewsbury.

Commemorative windows in the Central Library, Birkenhead.

MY SUBJECT IS WAR AND THE PITY OF WAR

120

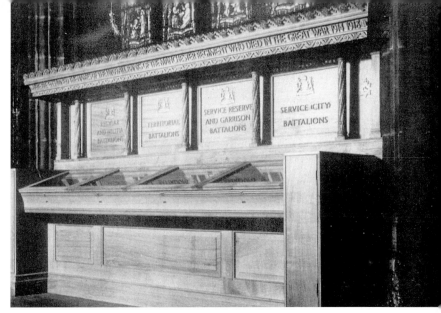

Manchester Cathedral: the Manchester Regiment Chapel Roll of Honour.

Oswestry: the Broad Walk next to St. Oswald's Church, where Tom and Susan Owen were married and Wilfred was baptised.

LIEUTENANT
W. E. S. OWEN, M.C.
MANCHESTER REGIMENT
4TH NOVEMBER 1918 AGE 25

"SHALL LIFE RENEW
THESE BODIES?"
OF A TRUTH
ALL DEATH WILL HE ANNUL W.O.

FUTILITY

Move him into the sun—
Gently its touch awoke him once,
At home, whispering of fields half-sown.
Always it woke him, even in France,

Until this morning and this snow.
If anything might rouse him now
The kind old sun will know.

Think how it wakes the seeds—
Woke once the clays of a cold star.
Are limbs, so dear achieved, are sides
Full—nerved, still warm, too hard to stir?
Was it for this the clay grew tall?
—O what made fatuous sunbeams toil
To break earth's sleep at all?

122

Bibliography

The Poems of Wilfred Owen, ed. Edmund Blunden, Chatto & Windus, 1931

Wilfred Owen: A Critical Study, D. S. R. Welland, Chatto & Windus, 1960, 1978

Wilfred Owen: Collected Letters, ed. Harold Owen and John Bell, Oxford University Press, 1967

Journey From Obscurity, Harold Owen, Oxford University Press, 1967 (3 vols.)

Wilfred Owen: A Biography, Jon Stallworthy, Oxford University Press/Chatto & Windus, 1974

The Poems of Wilfred Owen, ed. Jon Stallworthy, The Hogarth Press, 1985

Wilfred Owen: Selected Letters, ed. John Bell, Oxford University Press, 1985

Owen the Poet, Dominic Hibberd, Macmillan, 1986

Journey from Obscurity, Harold Owen, Oxford University Press, 1988 (1 volume, abridged from original)

Wilfred Owen, Anthem for a Doomed Youth, Ken Simcox, Woburn Press, 1987

Wilfred Owen: The Last Year, Dominic Hibberd, Constable, 1992

Wilfred Owen, Merryn Williams, Seren Books, 1993

Wilfred Owen's Voices, Douglas Kerr, Oxford University Press, 1993

Wilfred Owen, Soldier and Poet, Helen McPhail, Wilfred Owen Association/Gliddon Books, 1993

Siegfried Sassoon: Diaries, 1915-1918, ed. Rupert Hart-Davis, Faber & Faber, 1981

Collected Poems 1908-1956, Siegfried Sassoon, Faber & Faber, 1961

The Complete Memoirs of George Sherston (Memoirs of a Fox-Hunting Man, Memoirs of an Infantry Officer, Sherston's Progress), Siegfried Sassoon, Faber & Faber, 1937

Siegfried Sassoon, the Making of a War Poet: a Biography 1886-1918, Jean Moorcroft Wilson, Duckworth, 1998

Goodbye to All That, Robert Graves, Jonathan Cape, 1929

Up The Line to Death: The War Poets 1914-1918, ed. Brian Gardner, Methuen, 1964, revised 1976

Poetry of the Great War, An Anthology, ed. Dominic Hibberd and John Onions, Macmillan, 1986

Heroes' Twilight: A Study of the Literature of the Great War,

Bernard Bergonzi, Macmillan, 1965, revised 1996 (Carcanet)
The Great War and Modern Memory, Paul Fussell, Oxford
University Press, 1975
Regeneration (1991), *The Eye in the Door* (1993), The Ghost Road
(1995), Pat Barker, Viking
To What End Did They Die, R. W. Walker, Walker Publishing,
1985
The Register of the Victoria Cross, This England Books, 1988
The Sky Their Battlefield, T. Henshaw, Grub Street, 1995
A Companion to the British Army 1550-1993, D. Ascoli, Book Club
Associates, 1984
T*he British Base Camp at Etaples 1914-1918*, Douglas Gill & Julian
Putkowski, Musée Quentovic, Etaples, 1997
Public Record Office, Kew, WO95.562, WO95.2392, WO95.2397,
WO 138/4
Commonwealth War Graves Commission, Maidenhead
*The Regimental Roll of Honour & War Record of the Artists'
Rifles*, Howlett & Son, 1922
Birmingham Heroes, J. P. Lethbridge, Newgate Press, 1993
History of The Devonshire Regiment, 1914-1919, Ling 1932
The Devonshire Regiment 1914-1918, C. T. Atkinson, 1926
History of the Dorsetshire Regiment, 1914-1919, Ling, 1932
*The Story of the Fourth Army in the Battles of the Hundred
Days, August 8th to November 11th 1918*, Major General Sir
Archibald Montgomery, Hodder & Stoughton, 1919
The K.O.S.B. in the Great War, Capt. Stair Gillon, Nelson 1930
The History of The Lancashire Fusiliers 1914-1918, J. C.
Latter, Gale & Polden, 1949
History of The Manchester Regiment, vol.2, H. C. Wylly, Foster
Groom & Co. Ltd., 1925
*Manchester City Battalions of 90th & 91st Infantry Brigades
Book of Honour*, Kempster & Westropp, Sherratt & Hughes, 1917
The History of the Prince of Wales' Own Civil Service Rifles,
Wyman & Sons Ltd., 1921
T*he History of The South Wales Borders 1914-1918*, C. T.
Atkinson, Medici Society Ltd., 1931
History of the East Surrey Regiment, vol. 3, Pearse & Sloman,
Medici Society Ltd., 1924
History of the 15th Bn. The Highland Light Infantry, T.
Chalmers, McCallum & Co., Glasgow 1934
History of the 16th Bn. The Highland Light Infantry, T. Chalmers,

McCallum & Co., 19930

Breaking the Hindenburg Line. The Story of the 46th (North Midland) Division, R. E. Priestley, T. Fisher Unwin Ltd., 1919

Artillery and Trench Mortar Memories, 32nd Division, R. Whinyates, Unwin Bros. Ltd., 1932

Stand To! The Journal of the Western Front Association, No. 50, Sept. 1997

History of the Great War. Military Operations in France & Belgium 1918, vol.5, Edmonds, IWM, 1993

The Cross of Sacrifice, S.D. & D.B.Jarvis, Roberts Medals Ltd., Reading

British Regiments 1914-1918, E. A. James, Samson Books Ltd., 1978

General Index

V o4S 50

Index of Poems